INTIMACY REDEFINED

How God Can Assist You in all Your Relationships

Leslie Stancoven

Copyright © 2021 by Spiritual Lodestar

Copyright © 2020 by Leslie Stancoven

Published by Spiritual Lodestar

P.O. Box 911352 Nauahi ST

Waialua, Hawaii 96791

SpiritualLodestar.com

Cover design- Rob Williams ilovemycover.com

Photo credit: Erin Montante

Spiritual Loadstar Logo: Jamie Swim jamieswimart.com, "Lamp on an Island Black and White with Name"

Copyright © 2021 by Spiritual Lodestar

Editor: Robert Banks

Copyeditor: Jessie Raymond

Format: Auheduzzaman

Nihil Obstat:

Rev. Mark J. Gantley

Censor Librorum

Imprimatur:

✠ Clarence Silva Bishop of Honolulu

March 12, 2021

Library of Congress Cataloging-in-Publication Data

Stancoven, Leslie.

Intimacy redefined : how God can assist you in all your relationships Leslie Stancoven.

ISBN 13: 978-1-954691-00-1 (Paperback Edition)

ISBN 13: 978-1-954691-01-8 (eBook Edition)

ISBN 13: 978-1-954691-02-5 (Audio Edition)

Library of Congress Control Number: 2021903726

First Printing: December 2021

All rights reserved. No part of this publication may be reproduced, distributed, or transmitted in any form or by any means, including photocopying, recording, or other electronic or mechanical methods, without the prior written permission from the author, except in the case of brief quotations embodied in critical reviews and certain other non-commercial uses permitted by copyright law.

The sample stories in this book are fictitious, and were told to emphasize a point. Any similarities to actual persons, either living or dead, is coincidental.

The author of this book does not dispense medical advice or prescribe the use of any technique as a form of treatment for any physical or medical problems without the advice of a physician, either directly or indirectly. The intent of the author is only to offer information of a general nature to help you in your quest for spiritual and emotional well being. In the event that you use any of the information in the book for yourself as your constitutional right, the author and the publisher assume no responsibility for your actions.

Who should read this book?

Do you feel called to take a closer look at your relationships? Are you searching for more meaning and satisfaction in your life? This book is for anyone who desires more intimacy in their relationships, anyone who feels like something is missing from their life, and anyone interested in pursuing new intimate relationships. The meaning of the word, intimacy, is so much more than what is typically thought of in our society. We will explore what intimacy truly is as we redefine intimacy in our relationships, enabling us to live the best quality of life.

Throughout this book, we will redefine our intimate relationships by inviting Christ into our lives. As our relationships evolve, in turn, our lives will regain more purpose, meaningfulness, and satisfaction. As you read this book, you will learn how to grow your intimacy with God, as well as with others. You will discover what is necessary for increasing intimacy in existing relationships, and how and when to create new relationships. Finally, you will understand the importance of establishing new, steady ground for all of your relationships to have the opportunity to flourish. As you focus on growing your intimacy with God by placing your trust in the Lord, achieving a redefined intimacy with God and your loved ones is closer than you think.

Acknowledgments

Thank you God, Jesus, and the Holy Spirit.

To my husband, Brian, thank you for your loving support. Thank you to my parents, Ron and Monica, and my in-laws, George and Bonni. Many thanks and gratitude to all of my friends, family, and mentors who have helped me on my journey.

A special thank you to all the institutions that assisted me in obtaining information for this book, especially during the COVID-19 Pandemic:

John A. Burns School of Medicine Health Sciences Library

The Office of the Bishop, Roman Catholic Diocese of Honolulu

Sueltenfuss Library at Our Lady of the Lake University in San Antonio

The University of Hawaii at Manoa, Hamilton Library

TwleveWeekBook.com and Dr. Richard Nongard

About the Author

Leslie Stancoven started out with a Master of Science in Marriage and Family Therapy, as well as a License in Professional Counseling. She has provided counseling for individuals and groups in many different life transitions. She is a world traveler and has lived many places around the world as a military spouse. When Leslie is not writing, she enjoys hiking, reading, and spending time with her family and church community. She is a mother of three daughters and a cat lover.

Visit SpiritualLodestar.com for more information.

Other books by Leslie Stancoven:

Intimacy Realigned:
Marriage Maintenance Through Christ
(expected release October 2022)

The State of Intimacy: Achieving Intimacy
Through the Art of Poetry
(expected release January 2023)

Intimacy- a closeness; a friendship or mutual bond.

(New American Oxford Dictionary)

Table of Contents

1. Finding God 1
2. Invitations Aplenty 15
3. Ladders, Anchors, Volcanos… Oh My Redefined Intimacy! 22
4. Semantics Vs. Politics 51
5. Forgiveness 64
6. Trust, Love, Friendship, and Marriage 76
7. Terms of Commitment 85
8. Prayer 92
9. Community 98
10. Best Version of Self for Redefined Intimacy 105
11. Peace, Love, and Goodwill 112
12. New Ground and Future Blessings 123
Bibliography and Suggested Reading 129
Glossary 131

1
Finding God

Difficult things are best said with love. That being said, I have something to say. If we do not develop an intimacy with God, we have nothing in this life. No matter how many friends and family we have, no matter how much wealth and health we have, we have nothing if we do not have quality, meaningful, and intimate relationships that are based on the Word of God and our life purpose. This is the type of quality relationship we yearn for in our hearts, as we aim to feel satisfied in life.

What quality of relationship comes to mind when you hear the word intimacy?

Intimacy is defined in most dictionaries simply as a closeness; a friendship or mutual bond. However, this definition of intimacy only touches the surface of what intimacy could truly entail; it is no indication of the depth and quality of what you will discover about intimacy as you read this book. What feelings come to your mind when you hear the word, intimacy? We will be redefining what true intimacy is throughout this book. Through quality relationships that God guides us to enter or maintain, we can help create meaningful and intimate relationships, one interaction at a time.

Romance

If you think about romantic intimacy when you hear the word intimacy, you are not alone. In our society, intimacy has become synonymous with romantic love. We see couples kissing and hugging, and we assume they have obtained intimacy. However, that is just what we conclude and often aspire to obtain for ourselves. Love, either romantic or non-romantic, is actually just the tip of the iceberg (or the volcano as we'll explore in Chapter 3). It is true that intimacy can be achieved with a romantic partner. A truly exclusive and intimate, deep connection, can exist in a romantic relationship. However, romance and intimacy are not the same.

You are not alone if your view of intimacy is synonymous with romance. However, if you have ever been in a romantic relationship and experienced loneliness, you may have realized romance and intimacy can in fact coexist, but they are not the same. You can also experience intimacy in other types of relationships as well.

Friendship

Let's explore intimacy in the context of friendships. When we hear the word intimacy, we should immediately think about a high-quality relationship, with the emphasis on quality, not quantity. This is very important here, and the Bible offers some guidance on friendship. The Bible defines friendship as having a close relationship or a bond; an important responsibility of the Christian faith. God wants us to experience high quality and intimate friendships, and He can guide us to these people on our journey of life.

Each of us has a checklist in our minds as to who, when, and what constitutes as an intimate friendship. Most people would say loyalty, trust, and having a common viewpoint are the foundations of a friendship, as well as any other intimate relationship. Individuals possessing these traits can help us build trust and love in relationships that have the potential for friendships and marriage. These are traits that we value in other people. Do you possess these traits? What other traits do you value in those you would call a friend or loved one?

In all relationships, intimacy occurs in the space in-between. The level of intimacy you are capable of reaching in a relationship is not solely determined by you. Regarding intimacy, each relationship we have is limited by the person in the relationship that has the lowest level of intimacy. Later in this book we will learn about rating our intimate relationships, creating new intimacies, and leaving an intimate relationship as an act of God's love.

Family and Our Village

In this life we are either born into a family or raised by guardians chosen for us. Our experiences in our home life shape our beliefs about the world as we develop from childhood into adulthood. In the traditional sense of family, our first opportunity to build intimate relationships is with our parents or caretakers and siblings. The family unit is the most basic union. Our village is an extension of our family unit.

Our modern-day village is populated by the people with whom we have daily interactions, both in person as well as virtually. These people have the potential to become a family in the modern sense of the word. On the other hand, if we are not mindful, many of these interactions can become devoid of intimacy. Intimacy is the answer to creating meaning in our lives. We now have so many possibilities with how we spend our free time and with whom we choose to spend our time. In our ever-changing, fast-paced, and overly saturated modern-day world, it can be easier to start a new relationship than to maintain an existing relationship. When we talk about our village, we can think about the people we come into contact with every day. Modern day villages may include our traditional family, modern family, friends, as well as our online community of social networks. How can we remain present and open to intimacy in this modern day village?

It has been said, it takes a village to raise a child, but what happens to the children we raise? As children, we hear fairytales that portray heroes fighting villains and living happily ever after. As adults, we realize life is not as neatly defined as a fairytale. There is so much more to the story of your life than reaching a magical age of adulthood, becoming all-knowing and living happily ever after. Life can get messy, and it takes a lot of maintenance. The story of your life is important. You are a part of a village, both global and local; everyone has a role to play.

Every villager is important. Every person has been created by God for a purpose. With the goal of building intimacy through meaningful relationships, we can all work together to achieve a larger goal of living better lives while we are here on this earth. While different societies have different ideas on how our villages should operate (and how governments manage them), it is important that we recognize that we are a part of a modern-day village, both global and local. We need to remain present in our lives, in order to be receptors and senders of intimacy. We need to decide what villages we are a part of, and then make an effort to not let the village become separate from who we are. How can we ensure we are a part of this ever-forming "village" and maintain intimacy in our lives?

Historically, villages were created for efficiency and safety. People within a village relied on each other for goods, services, and protection. As a member of a village, you relied on other villagers. With technology and the advancements of the modern day world, the reality is, some of us are much more in tune with the global village than our local village. Maybe we get our groceries delivered to our front door while we are working from home. As we are working from home, maybe we are conferencing online with a client or a coworker who lives two states away that we have never met. The 21st century has given way to a world of amazing technology. Unfortunately, this can cause a disconnect in many physical relationships. Nowadays, many people are immersed online; checking emails and social media, chatting with old friends and old flames. We may not be spending this valuable quality time with the very person who is sleeping next to us, or the friendly and thoughtful neighbor who lives next door. Our global village can be just as real as our local village. However, we may need to set foot in both our local and global villages to maintain intimacy in our modern-day life.

Our modern-day life's village includes who we spend time with, who we rely on, and ultimately how we spend our energy. What type of village do you live in? Is it both global and local? Do you have a presence there? What would someone say about you if asked what type of person you are, based on the things that you say and do? In Chapter 4 we will discuss how the things we do and say are based in our own belief systems. You will also learn how what we say and do brings meaning to our conversations, and ultimately our intimate relationships.

We can choose to be present in our local village. When we go to the grocery store, when our mail is delivered, when we walk down the street, let us choose to be present with the people we see. Let us offer peace, love, and goodwill to our village, creating opportunities for union and friendship.

We can choose to be socially responsible with the capabilities of widespread, highly-charged emotion in the arena of the global village. When we respond to messages on our social media, let us offer positivity with our posts and replies. If we disagree on a thought, behavior, service, or product—whether in person or online—let us know when to constructively intervene, and when to walk away.

Let us be present, kind, offering constructive thoughts and actions, and aware in our village in all that we say and do. How can we be present in all we do? In Chapter 2 we will explore how to invite God to take part in all we do. Living life for God's will is the answer to becoming better conduits and receptors for intimate and meaningful lives. In Chapter 6, we will discover how focusing on a feeling of gratitude can both help us feel present as well as encourage being an active member of the village that we live in.

How can we change our relationships within our village? When service workers come to our house to check our electrical meters, let us feel grateful that they are performing this service, so we do not have to do everything and be everything in our village. If you see that someone is crying on a park bench, ask God if you should reach out to them. By asking them if they are ok, we recognize that they are a part of our village. By taking on the responsibility of living in a world that we want to live in, we can help create a meaningful and intimate reality, one interaction at a time.

How can our relationships become more intimate? Are these the types of meaningful conversations you would like to have? Building relationships takes work. We can choose to build more intimacy in our lives. We can choose to be present in all we do. The payoff from doing this work is that we will benefit from the satisfaction that comes from gaining intimacy in those relationships. How many opportunities do you have in a day to have a meaningful conversation? How many opportunities do you have in a day to spread peace, love, and goodwill—radiating God's love to others?

A life without these intimate relationships is a life without purpose and meaning. How can we recreate our world with more intimacy, more meaningful conversations, more love and satisfaction? To learn the answer, we will practice using our intimacy tools, including the skill of listening, both to God and to others. We can listen to our village and pay attention to what is going on in the world around us. We achieve more intimacy in our lives by using the wisdom and understanding we learn from God as we choose to grow our relationship with Him. The social intelligence of pursuing intimacy with God is the missing piece of the puzzle in a satisfied and happy life.

Divine intimacy

Many of us live in a reality that is drained of intimacy. If we are not careful, our day can be filled with meaningless thoughts and actions. We can easily find ourselves in conversations about people that we barely know, or in relationships that are devoid of intimacy. Let us choose to seek out more intimacy in our reality.

The truth is, we are all alone in this world if not for the love of God. We all have this love, but like any relationship, we need to pursue it to reap the full benefits. I have a solution to your intimacy problem. This solution starts by redefining what intimacy means to you. As we change the meaning of intimacy and truly understand it, we will subsequently be offering it to our loved ones. As we incorporate intimacy building tools into our lives, we will be building stronger, positive-based relationships that will carry more depth and meaningful intimacy. In order to delve deep into our relationships, we must first look to find God.

Proverbs 8:17 ASV

"I love them that love me; And those that seek me diligently shall find me."

How will we find God? It is said that as we live in this world, each life is on a journey. If we think about God as the Creator of the world, but as a separate entity up in Heaven, it is easy to have a "me versus the world" attitude. While it sometimes may feel like that—like everyone and everything is against us—we can also acknowledge the Creator in all things. From this perspective, there is God (all-good, all-knowing, bringer of the Holy Spirit) and His adversary (devil, all things evil, passions and fears of the ego). From everyday tasks to life's biggest milestones, let us be sure that we invite God (the good) into every area of our lives and our relationships. Let us invite God's unconditional love into our hearts and have Him create the opportunity to share His love with others.

Are you happy with your current life, and the path that you are on? Do you wish to create more meaningful and intimate relationships? If our reason for living is to know God, love God, and serve God in this world in order to be happy with Him in heaven, let us not delay in living a life of **Christian servitude**. Christian servitude is devoting our purpose here on earth to serving God, by following the ways and teachings of Jesus. By setting out to achieve this goal, we will redefine intimacy in our lives.

If God were here right now, what would He say to you about your journey of life, your rights and wrongs? We all have rights and wrongs. As Christians, we can come to terms with this and recognize that we are all sinners. No matter what your sins are, I feel confident that God's gift of Jesus is clear, "I love you with all my heart."

1 John 4:9 ASV

"Herein was the Love of God manifested in us, that God hath sent his only begotten Son into the world that we might live through him."

It is easy to look at life's obstacles and see the mountain that we cannot climb, or the fault line that we just cannot cross. Imagine the early explorers who disproved the theory that the world was flat. They set out on a journey across the ocean, where they trusted that life and land was out there. These explorers trusted that no matter what was out there, they would live to tell the tale. They set off not knowing what they would find. Like those early explorers, or anyone who embarks on a voyage into unknown territory, we cannot see it until we set out on that faithful journey. Regarding intimacy, what can we do about the insurmountable problems, the feelings of being too small in a big world, and the feelings of loneliness and isolation as we continue on our journey of life?

As we begin our journey to redefine intimacy in our lives, we can recognize that we already hold certain beliefs. We were all raised with certain beliefs. Those beliefs happen in two ways—by what is said and what is done. Later, we will shed more light on this (semantics vs. politics). As humans, God gifted us with the ability to think and feel. We are capable of being life-long learners. Sometimes it is necessary to change a belief in order to adapt and change to life circumstances and situations. Let us endeavor on our journey to never be limited by our beliefs on our journey.

It is the ultimate goal of our life journey to be accepted into heaven. I long for an intimacy with Christ more than anything in the world. There is no worldly thing that can make me stay here if it is not for the will of God. As a Catholic and a Christian, I believe that the purpose of life is to have an opportunity to have a relationship with God through Christ. I believe that Christ is the mediator that God created for us to be closer to Him. I hope and pray for everyone to develop their relationship with Christ so that they can grow closer to God.

On our journey to redefine intimacy in our lives, we will learn how to become closer to others. Are you tired of wishing you were closer to your spouse or loved ones? Do you ever wonder what you could do to have closer, and more intimate relationships? What about those seemingly right relationships that somehow went wrong? If you desire more intimacy in your meaningful relationships, you are not alone.

What is it that makes friendships, marriages, and family relationships intimate? How is it that some fathers and sons get along, while others struggle to find common ground? How is it that some couples thrive together and make each other stronger, thereby building a bridge to new opportunities in their communities?

Think of your relationships. Is there one that stands out as being comfortable, equal in power and love, and leaves you with a feeling of happiness and satisfaction? Once you have this relationship in mind, think about how you achieved that sense of mutual intimacy. Furthermore, when you experience obstacles in this relationship, how do you get back up after a fall, as falls are inevitable? In other words, once you find common ground, how does the relationship withstand the test of time?

What if there was a secret key to achieving successful intimacy in your meaningful relationships? What if this key opens the door to obtaining, cultivating, and maintaining successful intimate relationships? Successful intimacy can be achieved with God and others through your relationship with Christ. Throughout this book we will be talking about how to grow our relationship with Christ in order to open other intimacy opportunities. We will also see how to use Christ as a compass throughout our journey of life—our journey towards a redefined intimacy with God and others. After all, without the experience of intimacy and meaning in this life, we would be left in loneliness and despair.

Sally's Story of Finding Happiness

Sally sat in one of several stalls of the ladies restroom in her office building, staring up at the tiny decorative pin holes of the perforated tiles. She wasn't even going to the bathroom, but she felt more comfortable alone in this stall, than she ever did in the office where she worked. According to anyone's account, Sally had "made it" in the world. But if that were really true, why did she feel so unfulfilled?

Sally had many friends. She ate lunch with her coworkers every day, they shared recipes, good conversations, and attended parties together. They all worked really hard together to achieve a common goal, and they were good at what they did. For many years, Sally also played on a league softball team, and she traveled around with her dugout buddies. When they weren't playing ball, they would often get together for dinner and even go camping some weekends. Sally even got together with some of her girlfriends from high school.

Sally kept herself busy. She had her life's work, her friends, projects around the house, and commitments in the community. Despite her professional and social success, at the end of the day, Sally could not shake the feeling of emptiness inside her. Sally thought about what she wanted to achieve in the future, and thought, "Maybe after that happens, I will finally be happy."

Sally came from a loving family and had grown up attending church. She believed in God, and prayed often to God, Jesus, Mary, and even the Saints. She wondered if other people were happier than she was. She even tried medication for depression, but she still felt unsatisfied and lonely, as if a hollowness was growing inside of her. No matter what she tried, nothing seemed to fill the emptiness and satisfy her.

One day many years later, Sally finally found her fulfillment. It was as though someone had turned on a light in a dark room. The hollowness was replaced with an understanding that there was a love for her greater than anything she had ever imagined.

Sally had many more successes and failures throughout the years, but as she continued to grow in wisdom and understanding, her perspective on the purpose and meaning of life had changed. She understood things in her 40s that she never understood while in her 20s, and so on. She was finally happy, but what had changed? Sally had recognized the emptiness inside her heart and she filled it with the only thing that can fill it—Christ's love. By choosing *to grow her intimacy with God, Sally's perspective on all of her other relationships changed. She was now able to cultivate and experience more meaning, purpose, and satisfaction from all of her intimate relationships. Sally had found the secret key to achieving successful intimacy.*

You may be thinking, "How was Sally able to find this love?" Sally chose to grow her intimate relationship with Christ. We all have this opportunity every day. Sometimes, we make a choice that leads us away from God, but we always have the opportunity for union with God. It's always easier to see our errors when we look back at where we have been and know we should have gone a different route. Returning to union with God means we can choose to bring God with us on every step of our journey, even if we had left Him behind somewhere along the way.

As we place our trust in growing our intimacy with God on our journey, something amazing happens. Feelings of emptiness, despair, and loneliness are replaced with fulfillment, hope, and meaningful and satisfying intimacies. By redefining intimacy through faith in Jesus, we will begin to cultivate peace, love, and good will.

Are you with me on this journey to redefine intimacy in your life by finding God through Christ? Our destination is finding intimacy with God and bringing God's wisdom and understanding into all of our relationships. Like the early explorers of our world, we are setting off from the docks right now on a journey across a vast ocean where we do not know what we may encounter. It is exciting to know that as we experience this amazing voyage to redefine intimacy in our lives, we will become more and more in sync with Christ. If you feel left behind, it's not too late. Jump aboard as we set sail across this ocean. Together we will dispel all fear, chaos, hostility, and hate on this journey to grow closer to God and others through Christ.

2

Invitations Aplenty

Proverbs 18:24 ASV

"He that maketh many friends doeth it to his own destruction; But there is a friend that sticketh closer than a brother."

The importance of intimacy in our lives is real, and in a fast-paced world it is often easy to overlook. We have so many things that grab our attention. Sometimes we forget to slow down and really invest ourselves in God. God created us through His love, and He gives us all the opportunity to live meaningful lives. We are all invited to get to know Him. By growing with God and getting to know Him intimately, we have the opportunity for meaningful **union** and intimacy along the way.

As we begin to search for intimacy in the world by increasing our intimacy with God, we can liken this task to many different metaphors. The metaphor for the Christians' journey has taken many popular forms: the journey, the path, the road, the quest, the Christian direction. In the Bible, we are told that all are invited to the table of plenty, the tree of life, and the fruit of the vine. There are many books and tutorials on how to achieve a closer relationship with God. As we attempt to redefine intimacy on our journey to get to know God, I will continue to liken our Christian journey to sailing across a vast ocean on a vessel.

We are traveling across a vast unknown ocean (our intimate relationship with God). We are each offered a vessel (Jesus Christ) in order to progress towards our end goal of getting to know God and finding something important along the way (redefined intimacy in all our relationships). Let us recognize this jump aboard our vessel as a leap of faith—something we cannot see or touch, but we can feel it in our hearts and "just know" that it is the right choice. Some passengers jump onto their vessel right away, eager to get closer to God. Others jump off the vessel and try to swim on their own. It is a noble effort, but not the most efficient way. Those who try this will at some point need to get back onto their vessel, as they tire out quickly in the water. Some take the leap of faith after excited encouragement from their loved ones and community of believers. Others are slower to warm up to the idea, carefully contemplating how this will effect them due to various reasons, or fears. We are already on board our vessel. We are waiting for the others standing on the dock, ensuring them that their vessel is here waiting for them, even though they cannot see it.

Everyone has the same opportunity here—to make the choice to come across this ocean to gain intimacy with God and others on the journey. However, not everyone will make the same decision as you. You have made the decision to take your vessel out into the ocean, and with faith, you believe you will reach a better place through believing that Jesus will bring you to the Father. You yearn to get farther out there in the ocean—

closer to God! As you feel the joy in your heart, you look around you in hopes of sharing your joy!

As you look around to see who can share this intimate journey—this intimate leap of faith—you realize that the farther you go towards where you know in your heart God wants you to venture, there are not as many other people. Not only that, but some dear loved ones are missing! You look back. You can see them still standing on the dock. Maybe they have a sorrowful look on their face, or perhaps they look like they are having the time of their life. What will you do? Will you go back?

Should you call out to them? What about your friends and family who have chosen to stay on the dock rather than pursue intimacy with God? Before you leave your vessel and swim back to the dock, remember that each person has the same opportunity. We all have access to our vessel, as we all have the opportunity to set out across this ocean to find God. Some will take their vessel into the ocean; some will try to swim on their own. Others may wait apprehensively on the dock, until it is the right time for them in their own life and way. Each vessel God gives us is only big enough for one person.

Trust in the Lord. Everyone is invited to cross this ocean to get to know God. These are the times to pray. Trust God to send Jesus to warm your heart. Trust Jesus to guide you when to leave and when to stay, when to speak and when to hold your tongue. Give Jesus full navigation over what you do and say. By doing so, you increase your intimacy with everyone God guides you to know and everyone God guides you to meet.

The feeling of leaving a loved one behind is difficult to think about. However, once you decide to get to know God, you are now going in a different direction from the people who stayed behind. Bridging the gap at family gatherings, at work, and in dying friendships can feel difficult. With love, ask the Lord, "What can we do if our loved ones have not yet decided to take the journey to get to know God intimately?"

On this journey to develop our intimacy with God, we will bring meaning and purpose to our lives. Deciding to take the journey, we are all inviting Christ into our hearts. We are going to purposefully work to invite God into all areas of our lives and into all of our works. Think of someone you love, who you seem at odds with—your friends and family that have yet to head out over the ocean? What can you do now to increase intimacy with your loved ones who are still on the dock, or those who are walking away from the Lord?

If someone is not with you, you can recall all the ways we attempt to cultivate intimacy in our relationships. We can shout out to those who are not with us on the journey. We can remind them and assure them that all are welcome on this journey. We can smile warmly and say nice things. We can continuously maintain our relationship with calls, texts and emails, and friendly gatherings. We might do these things over and over again. Sometimes we may succeed, but what do we do when our friends, neighbors, coworkers, and family have clearly chosen to stay behind?

Is there someone in your life whom you have worked truly hard to win over to the side of the Lord, but to no avail. Throughout our lives, there are those who are with us on our intimacy journey to get to know God, those whom God directs us to help redefine intimacy in their lives, and those that we need to respectfully leave be. As we continue to accept God's invitation for intimacy, we say, "Lord, whom can I help today; Lord, how can I serve you today?"

On our faithful journey across the ocean, the goal is to develop a redefined intimacy with God and others. We begin to realize something about our life decisions. We learn that as we continuously strive to be one with God's Will, we are actually allowing Christ to guide us. When God makes the judgment calls, we can then use discernment sent to our hearts by Jesus. Therefore, we learn that by following God's Will, we have the opportunity to gain intimacy with God, and we can help others to do so as well. Let us take a moment to search our hearts and ask the wise question, "God, do you call on me to help this person?" As we learn to do this, we can redefine the intimacy in our lives, restoring purpose and meaning. When we have given Christ full navigational control of our vessel, we are asking God to make those difficult decisions about our loved ones for us. We follow God by allowing Jesus to navigate our vessel. Think back to the people who chose not to make the leap of faith into their vessel.... Did we really leave them?

We are taking a journey to get to know God, and we can also envision that once we set out to achieve that goal, we can reach a new land and become planted as a part of God's plan. We can become a fruitful tree in God's forest of life! In this healthy, abundant, and fruitful forest, every seed God plants is one that flourishes into a vigorous tree. The only way to ensure that the we flourish, or ripen, is to follow God. Jesus leads us on our journey, and God plants us and nourishes our tree. Without God, the tree will ultimately die and be chopped down to fertilize His other, more fruitful trees. That goes to say that sometimes, the Lord may guide us to teach others, and sometimes He may guide us to hold our tongue. All are invited to journey to get to know God and become a thriving, fruitful tree, but not all will accept the invitation.

Have you noticed something about Christian metaphors—the journey, the path, the road, the quest, the Christian direction, and setting out on a vessel on a vast ocean? These are all ways of expressing the difficulty involved. There is a lot of work involved in creating an investment, growing a thriving tree in a plentiful forest, ripening fruit, and having the courage to take a leap of faith. As we grow our relationship with God through Jesus, these metaphors take on a greater meaning.

This greater meaning develops as our intimate relationship with the Lord develops. As we attempt to redefine intimacy in our lives, we are making a decision to actively talk to the Lord our God, as well as to actively listen to Him. **Active listening** is listening with the intent of understanding. Your relationship with God is THE most important relationship of your life. God is the reason we live and breathe. Why else would we have come into life if not to serve the Lord? We will explore this idea of **Christian servitude**—serving the Lord and others God guides us to serve—later in this book. God has unconditional love for all of us, and He wants to have a relationship with us. However, we cannot have a relationship with the Lord until we accept His invitation to have the relationship.

Do you desire to truly get to know the Lord our God, and truly connect with Him is a special kind of relationship? Do you hope for an emotional closeness between you and the Lord? As we desire a close personal friendship with the Lord, our desire to actively get to know Him and serve Him co-creates our redefined intimacy. Relationships are two-way, requiring both you and your loved one to be invested. Relationships become stuck or stalled when there is a mismatch in intimacy, but ultimately, all relationships are defined by the person with the lowest amount of intimacy invested. Look at your vessel on the vast unknown ocean of intimacy. Are you still close to the dock, or are you invested in the journey to redefine intimacy in your life by getting closer to God? Wherever you are on your journey across the intimacy ocean, God will meet you there. It is up to us to venture further across the unknown ocean as we decide to continue to increase our intimacy with God and those to whom God guides us.

Are you invested in getting to know God? How intimate are the current meaningful relationships in your life? These are both important questions we will contemplate as we discover the depth and meaning of the word—intimacy. In the next chapter, we will explore the levels of intimacy and the purpose they serve in your relationships, as we continuously invite God to redefine intimacy in our lives.

3

Ladders, Anchors, Volcanos... Oh My Redefined Intimacy!

Intimacy has many different levels, layers, and depths. In our lives we have several opportunities to explore intimacy within the context of different relationships. We organize these relationships into a hierarchy of importance throughout our lifetime. For example, as a child, you most likely held a higher level of intimacy with your parents or caretakers. Perhaps, you had a childhood friend with whom you shared your dreams and fears. As we grow into adulthood, God gives us opportunities to make lifetime commitments and create the most intimate relationship on earth through either marriage or ministry. We can also choose to become parents or guardians; a great opportunity for creating intimate relationships with our children and grandchildren. We can use several different metaphors to help us understand each individual intimate relationship in terms of levels, layers, and depths.

Ladder Metaphor

Christian minister and author, Beth Moore, suggests in her book, *Sacred Secrets*, that each person in a relationship holds a ladder. Beth states that we can look at the different levels of intimacy like a ladder. Climbing this ladder is necessary to diligently seek the next level of our relationship with God and others. Think of this in the context of a friendship. The more we connect with our friend, the farther we go up the ladder. The same is true in our relationship with God, in the sense that, the more we connect with God, the farther we go up the ladder. Whereas God is willing to meet us at the highest rung, we are the ones that control our relationship by holding back our faith, trust, and love. Take a moment to have Jesus search your heart. How high do you climb on your ladder with God?

Let's take this idea of an Intimacy Ladder even further. Rather than each person holding a ladder, let us consider that each of our intimate relationships construct a ladder. Each relationship ladder has 2 sides—one side of the ladder represents you, the other side of the ladder represents the other person in your intimate relationship. Imagine your ladder has 10 rungs of intimacy connecting you to the other person. The ladder itself is your relationship, and the rungs are a way for you to reach a higher level of intimacy. Your intimacy must be matched on both sides of the relationship in order to construct each new rung and a sound ladder. In other words, we now have a scale of 1-10 in terms of each rung with its corresponding number. This signifies how high we climb on the Intimacy Ladder.

How can we construct our Intimacy Ladder with God? With unconditional love coming in at a perfect 10 on the Intimacy Ladder, God alone rests at this rung—a perfect 10. Jesus is ready to help us build every rung of the ladder to bring us closer to God. The only requirement for going up the Intimacy Ladder with God is the desire to **commune** with God through prayer. You may be saying, "How do I communicate with God?

Conversations are a two-way street!" and you may not hear anything in return. Let us reflect on some of our personal relationships in order to learn how to communicate with God and construct our Intimacy Ladder with Him.

We can use the Intimacy Ladder as a measurement for intimacy in all of our meaningful relationships. Casually greeting other people and engaging in everyday conversations can have a very low level of intimacy. These types of interactions can be examples of 1st or 2nd rung intimacies. As we continue to get to know someone, we ask them questions, and we learn from their responses how we are alike and different. We will consider this level of intimacy to be the 3rd rung on the Intimacy Ladder. There is also a crucial load bearing rung to establish in the ladder construction process that is mandatory. This mandatory rung cannot be constructed until a decision is made by both parties about the fact that they want to be in a relationship and establish more intimacy.

After we have obtained the mandatory rung for stability, we can stand on the 4th rung of the Intimacy Ladder. The evolution of the relationship continues as we make ourselves available in time, energy, and treasure. As time goes on, we encounter life experiences together and earn each other's trust. This progresses into a greater sense of love, and our friendship can develop further into higher levels of love and respect. This construction of our intimate relationships does not happen overnight. However, contrary to what many may believe, in our modern world we do not have to be there in person with someone to have an intimate relationship. The internet, telephone, and videoconferencing, are all useable tools in the cultivation of intimacy in our modern world when we are unable to meet person to person.

As we talk, or pray, to God, we know that although He is not physically there, He is with us in spirit. Prayers can seem one-sided, but God is truly there listening, and He appreciates your intention to reach out to Him and build an intimate relationship. If you continue to approach God and invite Him into your life, you may learn to listen in a way that allows you to hear what He has to say. Take a moment to consider the intimacy in all of your intimate relationships. Can you recall an intimate relationship in the time-line of your life that felt one-sided? Let us make the choice to increase our intimacy with God by asking Him to shed light on our current and past relationships. Holding the intention of inviting God into our lives allows Him to redefine the intimacy in all of our relationships. Walking with God in all of our relationships ensures meaning and purpose in our lives.

In the Bible, Jacob asked for a ladder to climb to get closer to God. In the New Testament of the Bible, we discover Jesus is the ladder. For the purposes of this book, the idea of the Intimacy Ladder features asking the Lord into our hearts at each rung of every ladder, cultivating intimacy with others to whom God guides us. The more we attempt to get to know the Lord Jesus, the higher we construct our Intimacy Ladders with Him. The more we connect with Jesus, the more we will get to know God and other loved ones on the same journey. We can continue to build Intimacy Ladders with the Lord and others every day by holding the intention to commune with God and remembering to involve God in every relational area of our life.

The Bible has many other metaphors to guide us on our Redefined Intimacy journey. How about the fruit of the vine and the mustard seed parables? The fruit of the vine prospers while the other vines are dead and cut away. How can we relate this to our own life? What does God wish you to cut away in your own life in order to focus on Him? The mustard seed is a parable in the New Testament, where Jesus talks to us about being planted in fertile soil. What does your soil look like? Is it rich, and therefore you are able to grow as a strong, successful plant? How often do you cultivate? What is the quality of your cultivation? If you feel that your plant is not flourishing, try replanting yourself in the truth that we are all sinners.

After we reflect on the reality that we sin, what are we going to do about it? How do we right a wrong? Let us continue to explore the rungs of the Intimacy Ladder in our relationship with God, and then relate them to other meaningful relationships in our lives. Let us always focus first on building our Intimacy Ladder with God, the most important ladder of all.

Intimacy Ladder

1st Ladder Rung- Recognize and Apologize For Your Sins

God does not expect us to be perfect. As we apologize for our sins and build our relationship with God, we come to this realization. We can use the following story about Aaron and Angela—two siblings playing on an average day in family life—to learn about the importance of accepting responsibility in a relationship.

Aaron or Angela, Who Is To Blame?

Aaron didn't do it on purpose. Well, not really. Sitting there, watching his baby sister cry about having her fingers stepped on was really annoying. "It serves her right," he thought, "for sitting in the middle of the walkway." He thought his mother would scold him, but instead, she got upset that little Angela was once again complaining and crying. Aaron began to feel bad for

Angela, so he went over and apologized to her. He gave her a hug and tried to comfort her. He apologized for stepping on her fingers. "It was an accident," he thought, "but it had still happened."

Siblings everywhere have similar situations. We could make a point for both Aaron and Angela in assigning blame. Angela was sitting in a walkway where people were bound to step on her. Aaron wasn't paying attention to where he was walking. This is how accidents happen. How many times do we make a similar complaint to God, assigning blame to someone else and neglecting to accept our own responsibility?

How many times have we admitted that we have done something, but rationalized it anyway? Once we recognize that we are playing a role in our lives, we recognize that everything we do is either with God or without God—there is no in-between. The things that are done without God are our sins. They are accidents, mistakes, or missteps on our ladder, relying on something other than God. However, we can apologize for our sins and continue to build our Intimacy Ladder by connecting with the Lord.

2nd Rung- Semantics vs. Politics in Meaningful Conversations

The future pursuit of a meaningful relationship is often decided at this stage as commonalities are sought out. This is the "getting to know you" phase of a relationship. What you say and do really does matter.

In fact, it is our thoughts that influence what we do and what we say in our everyday lives. Our beliefs are a very important, yet often overlooked, component of a meaningful conversation.

Most miscommunications among people occur due to not realizing or conveying how a thought process or belief has affected our behavior in interactions. To grow your intimacy with God, share your thoughts and beliefs with the Lord, with an open heart and an open mind. As you seek intimacy with others in your life, adopt an attitude of Christian servitude. Approach meaningful conversations with the intention of being a life-long learner, rather than already being learned.

3rd-5th rung- Stability Fostering Trust and Love

So, we continue the practice of confessing our sins and asking forgiveness in our relationship with God. We have made an effort to do and say the right things in our lives, in an attitude of Christian servitude and lifelong learning. We invite God to search our hearts and open the door to bring us closer to Him. Now what do we do? This is where our faith in the Lord can be life-changing. We must trust that the Lord is our Savior in order to progress up the Intimacy Ladder with God. Establishing the trust rung is essential and mandatory to moving to the next rung in our relationship with God.

When is it safe to establish trust and love in our relationship ladders with loved ones in our lives? We must trust that God will provide us with this discernment, and we must trust ourselves to hear it. Additionally, God can tell us what to do and say to repair our broken intimate relationships that He deems salvageable. Receiving the go ahead from God tells us which relationships to work on, and which relationships to let go with love. Later, we will discuss how to overcome the death of a relationship.

6th-9th rung- Higher Love

At this level in a relationship, we have gotten to know each other, decided we have common ground through meaningful conversations, and we can stand on a strong, stable, rung of trust. From trust, love grows. These higher rungs of the ladder are not for every relationship, and they are unachievable if the rung of trust is not strong. Fear not, if you desire more of this type of satisfying intimacy. Have complete faith and trust in the Lord to help you achieve these higher rungs of the Intimacy Ladder with someone whom God directs you.

While we cannot control other people, we can focus first on our relationship with God. God can show you the way to achieving higher love and more redefined intimacy in order to create the meaningful relationships in life you deserve. These higher rungs of the Intimacy Ladder can lead to experiences of great satisfaction on your life's journey. You can truly explore yourself when you share your beliefs and ideas in a safe, trusting, intimate, relationship on these rungs of higher love.

10th rung- Unconditional Love

This is the final rung of the Intimacy Ladder, and it is only held by God. God possesses unconditional love for all of us. No matter what we do, we cannot obtain this level of intimacy with other people in our lives because we are not perfect like God. However, we can ask Jesus to take us here, if we are able to climb up this far in our relationship with God.

Miscommunication Story- The Doting Wife

Ramona knew it was going to rain. She didn't need to see a weather forecast to know what her hips were telling her. Oh, the pain! She looked outside her window with apprehension. It had not started yet, but it would soon—she could feel it in the air. Ramona had to go to the grocery store today to buy all the ingredients for a cake she promised to make for her husband Adam's 50th birthday tonight. She didn't want to let him down; he never asks for anything except his favorite dessert on his birthday. She put on her usual smile, got her purse ready, and said in a sing-song voice, "I'm ready to go!" As she got into the car, she thought to herself, "I'll be alright as long as I don't have to do anything else today."

What do you notice about this story? Do you see Ramona as lying to herself, or do you see Ramona as being a trooper and getting the job done? How we see ourselves and what we tell ourselves about different situations effects what we say and do. In this example, Ramona decided that it was worth her secret pain to follow through with going to the store and making the cake for her husband, despite wishing for better conditions. This can be a successful tactic to get her through the day, only if her husband truly does not ask for anything else. She is already feeling overtaxed, working through her pain while donating her time and energy to a task she feels obligated to perform but does not feel like doing. What will she tell herself if her husband also asks her to make his favorite dinner or if an unexpected chore arises? Either her thought process or her actions will need to be modified in order for Ramona to continue to succeed in maintaining a positive attitude while celebrating this joyous life event.

Miscommunication Story- The Self-Centered Teen

Peter was trying to keep his cool as a teenager cut in front of him in line at the gas station. He was clearly waiting in line to pay. He couldn't believe that people could be so unaware, or worse, rude. As Peter's hot anger boiled up inside of him, a mother with three children two places back in the line yelled up to the front, "Hey the line starts back here." The kid turned around and went red in the face. Peter was amazed—the kid really didn't know. He walked to the back of the line and waited his turn. Peter wondered what the kid had been thinking about, as he had obviously not been aware of his surroundings. "That guy is so self-centered," Peter thought to himself.

In this scenario, Peter believed that kids do things because they don't know, or are being rude. Peter was surprised to see the look of embarrassment on the kid's face as he took his place at the back of the line. This may not always be the case. After all, we have all witnessed rudeness, but maybe next time this happens to Peter, he will decide to offer the person a chance to right the wrong.

Both of these miscommunications have something in common. They are both one-sided. What happens when we add another person into the reality? In other words, we are going to look at the same situation from another person's perspective. After all, relationships are two-sided.

Miscommunication Story- The Diligent Husband

Adam was the picture-perfect husband. At least that is what his wife always told him. Today was Adam's 50th birthday, and he was looking forward to a quiet evening at home with his wife, Ramona. Ramona always tried to go all out and plan a surprise celebration with their neighbors, friends, and family. It wasn't until their sons became too busy with their own lives that he finally got to do discover what he wanted on his birthday— absolutely nothing. Adam owns a family business and works almost every day. However, for the past 20 years he had been closing the store on his birthday. It was a big step for him to learn to relax, but he really looked forward to doing nothing on his birthday. He heard Ramona call out to him from the other room; She was ready to go to the store. He hoped Ramona didn't want him to do anything else today, but he didn't know how to explain to her that he wanted to celebrate by doing nothing.

In this scenario, we see that Adam actually does not want to do anything today, despite it being his birthday. Although Adam may have asked for a cake and probably really looks forward to eating it, he and Ramona actually want similar things—they both do not feel like doing anything today. Imagine the feeling of relief they could feel when one of them has the courage to share this similar interest and is made aware of their common ground. Relationships continue to develop trust when both people feel safe enough to share their feelings, no matter if they agree of disagree.

Miscommunication Story - The Over-Whelmed Teen

Justin was so nervous that he was going to be late. His uncle was on a layover flight from Chicago to Ontario, and he asked Justin to bring him some Illinois lottery tickets. The tickets were for Justin's grandmother in Ontario. Grandma Jones was a 98-year-old picture of health who loved to play the lotto! She was going to get a big kick out of the scratchers that Justin promised he would deliver to his uncle during his quick layover.

Justin had never actually bought a lotto ticket before, but he heard that they were at the counter. He walked into the store, scanned the shelves behind the cashier, and spotted them right away! He would make it to the airport on time after all! As he fumbled in his pocket for his wallet, he heard a lady at the back of the store yell, "The line starts back here."

Justin was buying a present for his grandmother, running late, and he was performing a new task he had never done before. Justin was embarrassed that he did not take into account the line of people waiting to buy things at the store. While it's not right to skip people in line, Justin was still able to right his wrong. Imagine if he had just left the money on the counter, or planned for this errand the day ahead. We all make mistakes sometimes. Hopefully, in the future Justin will recall the feeling of embarrassment and running late and plan accordingly for accomplishing his promises and commitments. Justin is young, inexperienced, and overwhelmed, but he does not seem to deserve Peter's title of "self-centered."

These stories were told with different perspectives to illustrate the point that we are all complex human beings. We all do things based on the beliefs we have about life as well as an experienced pattern of past events. The events may be real or imagined, and the perception of these events can differ from one person to another. While our loved ones may do things that we do not understand or upset us in some way, it is very difficult to put someone in a box with just one label. When you experience a miscommunication with a loved one—an argument—remember to invite God into the situation. If you feel guided to discuss a miscommunication with someone, take care to discuss the miscommunication in a constructive way rather than a deconstructive way. We will learn about constructive conversations in the next chapter.

Think about a miscommunication you have recently had with a loved one. We can use these everyday miscommunications from the stories in our own lives to become closer to our loved ones, and closer to Christ? Remember, when we have a conversation with Christ about what we need, want, or fear, He already knows. However, sharing these things with Christ opens up our hearts to receive messages from Christ, thus strengthening our intimate relationship with Him. We can strengthen our other intimate relationships as well in the same manner. We can use past miscommunications in our relationships as tools for constructing future intimacy.

Let us ask God to strengthen our intimate relationship with Him and others in our lives.

Dear God,

With the ultimate goal of knowing you intimately through achieving wisdom and understanding sent by you, please send Christ to search my heart. Please bring me closer to you, God. Please enter all of my relationships, increasing my intimacy with my loved ones and others whom you choose for me to know intimately.

Amen.

Anchor Metaphor

Let us look at increasing intimacy in a relationship in a different way. We started this journey to redefine intimacy in our lives by talking about getting into a vessel, and setting out on a vast, unknown ocean to find God. As we continue to discuss establishing intimacy with other people at different stages on their journey of life, we look to our vessel and find an anchor attached to a rope. On this journey to redefine intimacy, anchoring refers to Jesus asking us to take pause. Jesus can ask us to pause on our journey across the vast sea of intimacy toward God as well as toward other people. We look over the edge of our vessel, still holding on tight. Shall we let go of our rope and anchor our boat? Why did God ask us to pause our journey? Pray to the Lord during these times of pause in life and relationships. He will teach you, and as His student, you will learn.

On our life's journey to get closer to God, and bring meaning to our lives through our redefined intimate relationships, there will be times we will need to anchor our boat. **Anchoring**, or pausing our journey to learn an important life lesson, or allowing for growth of ourselves or another person, takes place as we get to know God. Anchoring is not the same as choosing not to take the journey. Rather, it is a time for patience and reflection. Different seasons of life require different periods of growth and reflection in our lives. This anchor metaphor takes into account that we are all lifelong learners on our life's journey, either pausing to reflect on what we have learned, or waiting to learn something new.

Intimacy deepens over time as we venture further out across the ocean of intimacy. As we decide to enter into a meaningful relationship, trust and love develop. We make the decision to pull our anchor up and keep going. Our intimacy increases within our relationship, and we have the opportunity to take our vessel far across the ocean, into the unknown. So how do we strengthen our relationship to God? The answer is simple—we must make the effort to get to know God. Everyone is invited; However, some will choose not to come.

John 14:26 ASV

"But the Comforter, even the Holy Spirit, whom the Father will send in my name, he shall teach you all things and bring to your remembrance all that I said unto you."

Mary Ann's Struggle to Juggle

Mary Ann was extremely tired. She had a long day at work. Really, it had been a great day. She had landed a promotion and a pay raise! Many people had thanked her and recognized her for a job well done. However, at the end of the day her job was far from done. She was at the peak of her career, and the the last thing she wanted to do was worry about what she was going to make for dinner. She knew that as soon as she walked through the door, "What's for dinner, Mom?" would be everyone's first question.

She would listen to all of her children talk about their day at school, as well as her husband's best and worst moments of the day. Sure, she would get her turn, and she knew everyone would be really proud of her. As she continued to juggle all of her life commitments, she silently wondered to herself, "When will I feel like I have done enough? What is missing from my life?"

In the story above, Mary Ann is juggling the responsibilities of being a wife, mother, and a working member of the community. Does this sound like a typical day for you? Do you often feel tired or under appreciated, no matter how hard you work? Our lives are full of responsibilities, and we choose to contribute to these responsibilities with either time, treasure, or energy.

As we grow up and into our community, we can discover and try on different roles. Many of us take on more than one role. We all contribute to our lives and communities in different ways, and every contribution is important. Our roles can change overtime as well. What roles are you currently playing in your life? Do you have a struggle to juggle these roles?

Many of us experience this struggle to feel happy and satisfied. Growing up, we are made to believe that if we earn enough money we will be happy. While it may be true that wealth equals stability, it does not equal happiness. What does it take in this life to feel happy, satisfied, and meaningful? Take a moment to assess what keeps you going in this life. We earn money in order to support ourselves and our family, and to purchase things that we need and want. Now, take another moment to ask another question, "Do you feel like all of your actions contribute something meaningful to God's Plan?" What needs to happen in order for you to feel accomplished in this life? For many people, meaningful and intimate relationships with God and others whom God chooses for you to be intimate, are necessary to help you feel satisfied and fulfilled.

Do you struggle to feel a sense of accomplishment, satisfaction, and fulfillment? Are you constantly searching for this feeling of completeness? Finding a balance between work and play is hard. Many of us chase after these feelings. We may chase these ideals in different ways. For example, we have competitions, awards, money, and the desire for better things in the future. Maybe you have won some of these things on your journey. However, above all else, I hope your journey brings you closer to God and others.

There are so many distractions on this journey of redefined intimacy in our lives. We have the ability to make a perfect meal ourselves or go out for our favorite meal. We can travel half way around the world to discover new and better ways of doing something. There are many different desires to search out and attempt to fulfill on a mission for happiness, satisfaction, and accomplishments. These can be both healthy and unhealthy. Ultimately, I argue that anything that pulls you away from your journey has become unhealthy for you. When unhealthy desires become habits that we crave—centering our time, energy, and treasure around—we are now defining addictions. This can happen so easily.

Are you waking up in the morning thinking about something or someone? Do you organize your day around receiving a self-satisfying reward? We all do and say things to help us get through the day or pass the time. However, whether or not something in your life has become unhealthy is already known to God. He knows if and when something is interfering in your relationship with Him or others. If you are ready for more intimacy with God and others in your life and you realize that a desire has become unhealthy, ask God to free you from these chains. Ask God to free you of any earthly desires or habits interfering with your ability to establish intimacy with the Lord and others.

Experiencing the sense of true satisfaction, joy, and worth in life can only come from one place—the presence of Jesus in our hearts. Strengthening our connection to God through Jesus fills us with peace, a sense of purpose, and unconditional love. Yes, the love is unconditional. It is true that no matter what we have done, God's love has always been there, and will always be there. When we are not focusing on God's love, it becomes more difficult to feel our worth. Let us work on redirecting our focus on God's love by strengthening our relationship with Jesus. Are you ready to lift up your anchor?

Dear God in the name of Jesus,

Please help me on my journey of redefining intimacy in my life by removing anything from my life that keeps me away from you. I look forward to getting to know you and others to whom you guide me. God's Will be done.

Amen.

Volcano Heart Metaphor

In the field of psychology, we talk about Freud's Iceberg Theory of the Mind. The theory states that our mind is like an iceberg, comprised of our conscious, preconscious, and subconscious thoughts. Freud's theory suggests only about 10% of these thoughts ever reach the surface, but our behaviors are determined by our beliefs. Freud continued to expand on this theory, and this philosophy was the catalyst for many theories to follow in the field of psychology and counseling.

When I think about Freud's Theory of the Mind, I imagine each individual iceberg, alone in the ocean of intimacy, with our cold earthly desires lurking beneath the surface. While the theory is important to the development of the field of psychology, I am much more at home when I think about creating meaningful conversations and rewriting the story of life. These techniques are housed in what are known as post-modern theories in counseling.

However, I cannot deny that the Iceberg Theory has resonated with me and my worldview. Perhaps, there are seasons of your life when the iceberg metaphor appeals to you as well, feeling alone and isolated, devoid of intimacy with others and craving your heart's desires. Can you relate to feeling selfish and having animalistic desires? Have you ever felt alone, like an iceberg in the middle of an ocean?

Instead of us looking at those times in our lives as an isolated iceberg constantly suppressing our desires, let's choose to look at ourselves as having an unfulfilled intimacy with God. In this view, our heart is a bubbling, active volcano with Jesus at the core, ready to lay new ground and connect us to others to whom God leads us.

What is a volcano? A volcano is a mountain that opens downward into a pool of molten rock below the surface. Pressure builds in this pool, a vacant cavity below the surface, until an eruption occurs. Observe your feelings and beliefs. In your volcano heart, you are driven by the desires of your heart to develop a redefined intimacy with God and others. The goal is to release the emotional pressure in the lava pool that builds in our heart, to come to the surface and lay new ground for a better version of ourselves. This release of lava from the heart, and laying new ground connects us with other hearts that are on fire for Christ as we continue our journey to get to know God.

Yes, God will lay new ground to connect us to other people. Is your heart on fire for God? You can choose to lay the groundwork for your redefined intimacy with God and with others by asking Jesus to ignite the lava pool in your Volcano Heart. There is no time like the present, so go ahead and invite God to do this now:

Dear God,

Please bring Jesus into my heart to bring me closer to you and others to whom you guide me on my journey.

Concentrate on building your Volcano Heart. Can you feel the lava running through your veins? Thank God for your experience of His pure and unconditional love as you say, *"Amen."*

Putting It All Together

We are all a part of God's Plan; we are all important to Him. God already knows you, but He also has the desire to be invited to get to know you. He wants you to make the choice to get to know Him as well. By taking determined steps to get to know God, you can increase your intimacy with Him, thereby creating a meaningful and purpose-driven life.

We can build our ladders, draw up our anchors to move our boats, and release our hearts' desires in a volcano of redefined intimacy, while living meaningful lives of Christian servitude with others. We can discover our worth as we redefine the intimacy and meaning in our lives by accepting God's invitation, allowing Jesus into our Volcano Hearts, and allowing God to build new ground for our redefined intimacy to flourish.

How do we get closer to Jesus? This seems like a simple enough question, and I bet you can already guess the answer. We can read the Bible, attend worship services and pray, practice meditation, and follow the Ten Commandments. Did any of these practices for communing with God come to mind? These are common ways that we have all heard about as ways to get in touch with Jesus. We know the answer, but now let us feel the answer in our Volcano Heart. Ignite your fire for Christ as you make a choice as to how you can best grow your intimacy with God at this time in your life. Follow through with your intentions to get to know God.

However, if we already know how to increase intimacy with God, what keeps holding us back? Someone once asked me, "Will Jesus recognize us when we die and go to heaven?" To which I replied, "Of course! God knows everything!" After thinking about how we get to know people however, I think the real question is; "When I die, and I am standing there with Jesus in Heaven, will I recognize Him?" Just because God already knows everything does not mean he doesn't appreciate the process of us choosing to get to know Him. How do we treat the people we love, and how do they know we love them? We choose to spend our time, energy, and treasure with them. Take a monumental moment—how much time, energy, and treasure are you spending on getting to know the Lord?

How do you rate your intimacy with Jesus and your loved ones? The following questions can help you assess your redefined intimacy in your relationships on a scale of 1-10, with a score of 10 reserved for God's unconditional love. As you go through the scale, think first of your relationship with the Lord, and then someone in your life whom you share intimacy. Give yourself 1 point for every time you answer "yes" to the following 10 questions:

Redefined Intimacy Scale

1. **Divine**: Is your relationship based on God's love? After searching your heart and asking God, you have discerned that this is an intimate relationship, and you will continue to redefine the intimacy within.
2. **Life Purpose**: Is the relationship supportive of your life purpose?
3. **Survives Change**: Life is full of change. Is this relationship accepting of life changes?

4. **Positivity**: Is this relationship based on positive ideals such as peace, love, and goodwill, rather than chaos, hate, and negativity? Emotional bonds are made stronger through Christ's love.
5. **Sense of Value**: Do you feel valued in the relationship when you do something good/succeed? You are given the space to fail, so that you can learn from your mistakes and become stronger.
6. **Constructive**: Is the relationship constructive? When sharing a difficult experience or life struggle, you focus on constructive solutions resulting in meaningful conversations rather than aimlessly complaining about life and problems.
7. **Trust**: Does the relationship have a strong bond of trust? The relationship is open and honest, free of manipulation. Any broken trust has been reestablished through the the Lord and the divine process of forgiveness. It is safe to open yourself up to become more intimate with this person in the future. *Be honest with yourself. If you are holding the relationship back, or anchoring, because of a lack of trust or a lack of common respect, subtract 2 points.*
8. **Love**: Can you give *and* receive a feeling of love in the relationship? You have an open heart with this person. *Mismatched intimacy or a breach of trust can result in a relationship that inhibits sending or receiving love. The relationship can develop into a closed-heart relationship, characterized by numbness, indifference, or hate. Subtract 2 points if you have closed your heart in this relationship.*
9. **Willingness to do inspired maintenance or leave the relationship as needed:** The Lord inspires this

relationship. Successful redefined intimacy requires either maintenance, including rekindling or anchoring, or letting go with love, as inspired by God. You are eager to pursue the necessary relationship maintenance. After you receive the go ahead from God to proceed with the redefined intimacy, you have a desire for increased intimacy or for restoring intimacy with this person.

10. **Reserved for God:** The perfect unconditional love that God provides for everyone. Only God can reach this level of perfection.

How high did you rate your redefined intimacy with the Lord? Have you discovered that you are anchoring or holding back in developing intimacy with Jesus? Now think about the person you are closest to right now in your life. Maybe this person is a spouse, a best friend, or a family member. How would you rate your redefined intimacy with this person? Now think about the Redefined Intimacy Scale in a different way. Ask yourself, "How high would Jesus and those whom I love rate our relationship on the Redefined Intimacy Scale?

As we attempt to analyze our relationships according to redefined intimacy, we may ask ourselves many questions. How often do you try to connect with this person and Jesus in your life? Are you and your loved one both present in this intimate relationship? Your intimacy interactions with Jesus may include prayer, attending religious services, or reading the Bible among other things. With a loved one, your intimacy interactions, or intimacy opportunities, might include text messages, emails, person to person meetings, even time spent thinking about being with that person.

I hope you have many opportunities to utilize your time, energy, and treasure with the person you are closest to right now in your life. However, I hope even more that the time, energy and treasure we spend each day cultivating our relationship with the Lord measures up to our earthly relationships.

We spend our time, energy, and treasure with the people we love. These are the outward signs of love. We do it in different ways. When you think about your love for those you spend your time, energy and treasure with, how does your relationship with Jesus measure up? If Jesus was standing before you today, where would your relationship fall on the Redefined Intimacy Scale? Would you compare your relationship with Him to the most intimate relationship you have or liken Him to a perfect stranger?

How close are you to Jesus? This is a much more difficult question to ask of yourself. Let's contemplate how we can recognize Jesus by starting with a cognitive behavioral question that we can quantify, "How many times a day do you try to connect with God?" "How many times a week?" Maybe you talk to God all the time, twice a day, once a day, once a week. Maybe you cannot remember the last time you have reached out and have simply fallen away from the habits of creating intimate opportunities with the Lord. Relationships are built between people, with each person playing a role. After assessing our intimate relationships with loved ones, we may now be able to determine how we would like to increase the intimacy in our relationships.

The first step to rekindling a connection is recognizing how intimate your relationship is and that you desire more intimacy. As an example, let's look at the goal of rekindling our relationship with the Lord to get closer to God. How can you achieve this? Is the answer simply to allot more time, energy, and treasure?

Continue to think about your current relationship with the Lord. This time, focus on quality time rather than the quantity of times you attempt to connect with Him. Which is more meaningful for you at this time in your life—five minutes of having the Lord search your heart or attending a church service? The answer depends on your state of mind and the season of your life. We are responsible for our role in the creation of our relationships. Steady your ground. Reassess your relationships, both here on earth and with God, using the Intimacy Ladder and the Redefined Intimacy Scale. Ask God for the best way to redefine intimacy in your relationship with Him and other loved ones in your present-day season of life.

We can continuously aim to see heart to heart with Jesus. When in doubt, start at the most basic level—recognize that we are not perfect. We can humble ourselves and recognize that we are sinners. Next, ask for forgiveness from God. Allow God to send Jesus to search your heart. By having a pure heart and good intentions, you are better suited for all of your relationships. You will be able to send and receive love, and experience intimacy on a much higher level. Along with trust, love is a requirement to increase intimacy in all of your relationships.

Remember, God is always present, and He represents one side of our Intimacy Ladder. In order for our ladder to be able to be used to bring us closer to God, we must be present in the relationship as well. To be a functional relationship, it's important to stand our ladder on a steady foundation. Therefore, let us be sure we are standing on the ground. What steps can we take to ensure our ladder is built on steady ground? What is the most basic thing we can say about ourselves?

Jesus has already said it when He recognized that we are sinners. Recognizing that we are sinners is indeed starting out on steady ground. By our nature, we all sin. Jesus died on the Cross to forgive all of our sins. He has paid the price, and now, through Jesus, we can all choose to do good. We can thank Him and make a fresh start every time our heart declares this.

How can we increase the quality of our time spent with those in our intimate relationships? Spending quality time with those we are intimate with can be achieved in many ways. For example, if you are geographically separated from your family, you can make the most of your remote interactions. Schedule a phone call at a time convenient for both you and your family. Choose to be present rather than distracted during the phone call. Remember that this is an opportunity to bond and increase intimacy.

How do we make a fresh start, create opportunities to remove our anchor, and move our vessels closer to God and others in order to increase our redefined intimacy? Let's say you decide to attend a church service—a great effort to obtain intimacy with the Lord. Imagine that rather than just being an attendant you become a patron to the church, sharing your time, energy, and treasure. As you share your time, energy, and treasure within a chosen community that you deem an important step on your intimacy journey toward God, you begin to develop friendships with other people within the community.

Creating the healthy habit of going to church service on your sacred day of worship increases the frequency of intimate opportunities with the Lord and others in the church community. We can increase our redefined intimacy within our church community just by creating this habit and holding the intention to connect with others to whom God guides us. However, choosing to not give precedence to the readings or the priest's homily is taking away from the purpose of attending the service. The world can be full of distractions, and the reality is that it is hard to be "switched on," both sending and receiving, all of the time. Say a prayer to ask God to help you focus on creating meaningful interactions with the Lord and others in your life.

Within your intimate relationships, sharing life's struggles are normal. One's desire for more intimacy constitutes a vulnerable state and a willingness to share our beliefs, truths, and these personal hardships. However, it is important to remember that most lasting bonds are fostered with positive ideals rather than negative problems. Consider the overall theme of your intimate relationships. Has sharing negative experiences and life struggles become a lasting theme in your life, but yet you still desire a deeper closeness with others? Ask God to reach deep into your Volcano Heart and bring Jesus into your relationships. When you invite God into your relationships, He will redefine the intimacy and help you create lasting bonds. In the meantime, the simplest behavior you can focus on to encourage a deeper intimacy with others is to offer more positivity to your conversations. Positivity is the best way to encourage growth of intimacy. If only life would stop getting in the way of our intimate opportunities!

Date Night for Bill and Sarah

Bill and Sarah have been dating for four years. They have accomplished many things while growing their relationship. Bill wanted to take Sarah out for a night in town and tell her how much she meant to him. He was feeling very sentimental and hoped to shower her with his love. However, all throughout dinner, Sarah was texting her colleague, as she was waiting for a big deal to go through. Unfortunately, after a two-hour dinner, Bill felt slighted. As much as he understood the need for Sarah to be available for work, Bill craved for more intimacy. He could not shake his disappointment, nor the fact that he did not feel satisfied emotionally. On the other hand, Sarah was grateful to have Bill's company at a time when she was feeling very anxious and excited. She felt bad for being poor company to Bill for the evening nonetheless.

This happens to all of us—we have the best of intentions, yet life gets in the way! Have you ever felt that an opportunity for building intimacy has slipped away, leaving you frustrated and craving more intimacy? You may have a similar story to that of Bill and Sarah. Feeling slighted and unsatisfied in a relationship can happen to anyone at any time. However, if this has become a lasting theme in your relationship, you may discover your relationship may be anchored until the time, energy, and treasure can be used to repair it. Choosing to anchor, rekindle, or let the relationship go are the different realities that we all constantly move toward in our relationships.

It is important that we learn to recognize these lost opportunities for intimacy and become honest with ourselves when we are not present in our relationships. This assessment process can allow us to ground ourselves so we can attempt to climb the Intimacy Ladder again. In all of our relationships, with the Lord and otherwise, how do we know the difference between the things that are helping us and the things that are hurting us?

Are you anchored in a place on your life journey to find God and get to know Him? Are you feeling stuck? What is the reason and how do you get unstuck? Wait, look! I see a bright lighthouse shining out on the water. We can look to this beacon of light for guidance. Are you too far away from land or others on this journey to see the lighthouse? Like the sailors used the stars, we too can find light even on the darkest parts of our journey. When we finally see the light, we can lift our anchor and confidently know which direction to travel next, progressing us on our journey to find God and redefined intimacy along the way.

Every time you decide to switch on your light, you become both a receptor to God and a sender of His light. God will show you the necessary tools for continuing your journey to redefine intimacy in your life. What do these intimacy tools look like? We have already begun to discover them on our journey. These tools include the acceptance of God's invitation, a commitment to the journey, prayer, and community. We will continue to discuss these intimacy tools later in Chapters 7, 8, and 9. First, we need to explore how to grow our redefined intimacy with God and others in the hierarchy of our intimate relationships through meaningful conversations in Chapter 4, the act of forgiveness in Chapter 5, and the importance of trust and love in our intimate relationships in Chapter 6.

4

Semantics Vs. Politics

From a counselor's perspective, clients come to therapy for help with a problem: "I'm unhappy," "I'm having trouble in my marriage," "I'm unsure about a life-changing decision." Part of the therapeutic relationship involves the counselor creating a safe space for helping their clients define their belief about the problem. This is also known as semantics. After defining the problem, the next step involves learning what the client is currently doing about the problem. This is known as politics. In, *The Construction of Therapeutic Realities*, Bradford Keeney, states that through talking about what the client believes and what the client currently says and does, we can construct outcomes in therapy and help guide the pathway for desired change or stability. We can learn from this formal therapeutic process and apply this knowledge to our close, intimate, and meaningful relationships. Using our own intimate relationships as a model, we can learn to create **meaningful conversations**, thereby building a redefined intimacy and our best reality possible.

On a daily basis, everything we do and say, our **politics**, are executed because of our beliefs and the meanings, or

semantics, we attribute to them. The concepts of semantics and politics are studied extensively in the field of communication, counseling, and other patient and client-driven professions. The intertwining and interrelation of these concepts of semantics and politics are the basis of many Post-Modern Theories of Counseling, including what are known as Narrative Therapy and Solution-Focused Therapy. The intertwining of these concepts creates our reality. Communicating in a certain way or choosing to speak about something creates either stability or change. In other words, we either continue the same story or start creating a new story. The story that we create, based on our beliefs, is our present reality.

Everyday, you accomplish tasks and duties with beliefs that may have begun as early childhood. As we mature, our beliefs expand, continue to evolve over time, creating an endless cycle of thoughts and actions. You may experience the same events as someone else, yet your reality may be different from these other people who have experienced the same thing. A basic example of this is an argument.

In addition to developing your own beliefs that began forming in childhood, you were also most likely influenced by other people's views, opinions, and beliefs as well. You create experiences and memories that can also shape your beliefs and reality. We create our ever-evolving realities every day in the story of our lives.

Think about the relationships in your life that you have identified as intimate. What is your current state of reality within these relationships? Would you identify the relationships as healthy or unhealthy, positive or negative? Maybe you have come to realize that your most intimate relationship has become one-sided, with either you or the other person doing most of the reaching out to connect. Take a look at the reality of the intimate relationship from your point of view, and then attempt to step into the reality of the other person.

As we continue to redefine intimacy in our current relationships, we can ask ourselves the following questions:

- Are you satisfied with the current reality of your intimate relationships on the Redefined Intimacy Scale?
- Do you think your counterpart is satisfied in this intimate relationship?
- Which is the highest rung you can both build on the Intimacy Ladder?
- Are you and your loved ones anchored on the same locations on your journey across the ocean of intimacy with God?
- How can we best serve the current relationship's purpose from an attitude of Christian servitude?
- How can we cultivate the redefined intimacy in our relationship to increase the meaning, purpose, and satisfaction in our daily lives?

We have been exploring the role we play in creating our own reality by attributing meaning to things that happen in our lives and then choosing either stability or change. What role has God played in your reality? Take a moment to reach out to God. Share your feelings and frustrations about your existing relationships in an intimate conversation with the Lord our God.

How are you feeling about your intimate relationships? Chances are you are reading this book because you recognize your desire for more intimacy in your life. Know that this missing intimacy in your life will come from God. Work to develop your relationship with God through faith in Jesus. God can heal existing relationships that He inspires us to maintain, and God can ignite new relationships that are inspired by Him.

We have the opportunity to establish trust, friendship, and love at any time in our lives. We meet many people everyday, yet these people that we meet, greet, and have conversations with may not climb higher than the ground level of intimacy. However, as our time spent with different people in our inspired relationships increases, and these relationships evolve, we become more comfortable with them, and our redefined intimacy grows. When we find the chosen few that God selects for us to share our life with, we feel safe enough to share our feelings, and at long last our beliefs, within the context of inspired, trusting, and intimate relationships.

New opportunities exist with the start of everyday to have meaningful conversations and increase the intimacy in our relationships. These intimate and meaningful relationships increase the satisfaction in our lives. You can choose to ask God to create this intimacy and make it your reality. As we trust that God will provide us the opportunity to live the best and most meaningful reality possible, we trust that Jesus will guide us to have meaningful conversations with those whom He guides us. Let us ask God to help bring more meaning and satisfaction to our lives through our intimate relationship with Him.

Dear God in the name of Jesus,

Thank you for blessing me with meaningful conversations to bring more intimacy into my life. Please continue to redefine intimacy in my life to bring more satisfaction, meaningfulness, and purpose.

Amen.

Many things can affect our reality. Our personality traits and temperaments influence our thoughts about life, both positive and negative. Our social environments and economic status effect our life. Our biological makeup, mental health and development, and season of life effect our reality. The culture of our family and community help shape our reality. Even the colors we choose to wear or decorate our homes with can influence our mood and therefore our thoughts. There are a multitude of stressors and entertainments surrounding us. There are thoughts in our minds affecting our moods. Our thoughts make up our belief system about ourselves and others; they influence what we say and do, creating the reality that we live in. It is clear; your reality starts with you.

When you think about the thoughts that make up your belief system, and therefore are a part of your reality, what do you tell yourself about you? Your thoughts about yourself may be positive or negative, constructive or deconstructive. As humans, we have all of the above. Happiness, freedom, and love are all positive things you can choose to focus on. Positive thoughts lend to more positive thoughts, thereby creating a cycle of positive thoughts. Likewise, when you are having negative thoughts and feelings about something, you can easily become caught in a negative thought cycle. Our thoughts create our beliefs, which influence our conversations and interactions with others.

Getting stuck in a negative thought cycle—why would anyone do such a thing? We have all experienced negative thoughts. You may be telling yourself, "I can snap out of it". I want you to know something that should not be discounted—your feelings are real. Like it or not, your feelings are a part of your reality. You should not pretend like you do not feel a certain way or that you have not experienced something. So how should we react when we have experienced something negative in life? A great loss, a breach of trust beyond what anyone would imagine, or a change of heart about a friend or a loved one can be devastating beyond words. In a world where we try to put our best face forward, suck it up, and keep moving forward, how can we constructively work through our pain and negative feelings?

Finding a balance of how to present yourself in a positive way, and staying positive in the face of life struggles can be difficult, if not overwhelming. When you are angry, how can you work through the anger and still present yourself as at peace to the world? How can you act happy when you know you are sad? How can you trust someone you love when they have acted in a way that is untrustworthy? Creating and maintaining peace and harmony in what we do and say everyday is easier said than done. However the ups and downs of your life—this reality—is the story of your life.

Does finding a balance between the reality of what is going on inside you, and what you present to the world seem difficult? That's because it can be difficult. The separation between your reality and what you want your reality to be creates a space. God longs to fill this space—to bridge this gap, and bring you into your best reality. The empty space is a weakness that must be filled.

The struggle to fill the empty space is real. In fact, this is so difficult that the struggle cannot be won on your own. Your struggle is a battle greater than you and the people in your life. How can we fight something that is greater than us? In the movie, *The War Room*, starring Priscilla Shirer, she does just that. Priscilla's character takes back the joy that the Devil had stolen from her, and she learns that she must choose a side in the greater war of God vs. the Devil. There are several books referencing this very real battle. Please see the suggested reading in this book such as, *The Battle Plan for Prayer*, or try an internet search of your own to lead you to further reading on this subject. These are modern-day examples I have found to describe our struggle as Christians in the world.

Your story is one of the many battles in the war between good and evil. Choosing to pick up your weapon—your prayers and trust in God—and fight, is the key to your satisfaction and happiness as you allow Jesus to fill the empty space between your reality and your desired reality. Choose to let God protect you from the Devil in your reality, and in the space between. Trust God to repair any gaps in your reality. God will bring you to your best reality and your best self.

God created the World, and Jesus is the King. The Devil is His opponent, the opposite of everything good that God created. The Devil is responsible for our fears that steal our joy and opportunities for intimacy. Take a moment to look at your life. Where can you ask God to come and strengthen your bonds of love? Where can God bridge the gap between your reality and what you want your reality to be, both healing your fears and increasing your intimacy.

What stands in the way of your intimate relationships? What limits you from reaching a level of higher love within your meaningful relationships? The Devil knows that when we are afraid, we cannot walk in God's love; fear is the obstacle that prevents us from entering into our best story of life possible. In the book, *Do Not Be Afraid*, Rabbi K.A. Schneider, explores overcoming these fears through Jesus. As God created the world, let us ask Him to create our best reality possible.

If you are unhappy with your reality and the story of your life, ask God to intervene and take over the battle for you. God can heal your fears. God can remove obstacles from your path. Have faith that God will be there for you in your times of need. When times of happiness occur within your reality, remember to give glory to God for your blessings.

If you could write the story of your life, especially if you are unhappy with the way it has been written so far, where would you start? If your battle is overwhelming, what should you do? When in doubt, choose a strategic retreat. The solitude of prayer can serve as a retreat from the struggles of life. A retreat can give your mind and body time to heal.

The word, retreat, may conjure up a "kumbaya" atmosphere with relaxing music and calming environment. When I talk about retreating, there is no need for a lavish location or elaborate procedure as we do not always have time for that. I am talking about prayer. The next time you recognize a negative thought pattern, take a moment and ask for God's help. Ask for Jesus to come to you and take this problem, obstacle, or fear. Ask for a solution, a way around, or the silver lining of the situation. Let us ask Jesus to bring us closer to God, by allowing our greatest friend "in" on our problem. God can reform our thoughts and help us regroup, reframe, or even rewrite our current life story. God can transform the story of your life from a tragedy to a triumphant survivor. Most importantly, God can remind you that you are not alone.

Saying a prayer to God in the name of His only son, Jesus, about your fears is the first step to bridging the gap in your reality of what you feel and what you present to the world. In other words, this is the first step in creating the best reality possible. Living an honest life of Christian servitude, where you have a redefined intimacy within your relationships, manifests the reality of living a life of meaning, purpose, and satisfaction that you now desire.

Mark 10:27 ASV

"Jesus looking upon them saith, With men it is impossible, but not with God: for all things are possible with God."

What do I mean by rewrite the story of your life to achieve your desired reality? Let us look at the following story of Carl and his grandfather. This story is an example of a life story viewed from different perspectives.

Realities Collide

Carl was a 12 year-old boy watching as his parents talked in whispers to his 55 year-old grandfather. He wanted to say something to reach out to his grandad. "He must be hurting." he thought. He had just lost the love of his life. Carl's grandmother had just died, very suddenly and unexpectedly. He knew his grandfather must be torn apart inside. After all, Carl knew how devastated he would be if one of his parents or if one of his siblings died. Carl thought, "It must be even worse to lose a spouse." Carl mustered up all the courage he had to reach out emotionally to his grandfather. As he walked into the room where his parents were sitting with his grandfather, Carl grew bolder and more determined with each step to offer his condolences. As he gently sat down on the couch next to his grandfather, Carl said the first thing that came to his mind. "Grandfather, do you think you will ever get married again?" Carl's parents gave a laugh, but to Carl's surprise, his grandfather laughed the hardest of all!

After the most heartfelt of laughs and with a sigh of relief full of love, Carl was sure he had said something inappropriate. His grandfather reached out his hand and placed it lovingly on Carl's knee. With a gentle yet firm commitment and rock-hard determination, Grandfather said, "No, Carl. I will never get married again!" Carl was stunned at the opposite of what he thought was going to be said. Dropping all pretense, he blurted out, "Why not?" Remembering his place, Grandfather just said, "Marriage is hard. You'll understand when you are older." Then he chuckled to himself and changed the subject. "Why would Grandfather say such a thing about my Grandmother?" thought the bewildered Carl.

Let us think about the story of Grandfather's life. This story is told from the viewpoint of an innocent observer—Carl, a 12 year-old boy. It was possible his Grandfather's reality, his story, had never been revealed to the family before. As listeners, we can think about cause and effect in relationships. We may wonder if Grandfather's reality was true or untrue. Upon hearing this story, we may even assign blame to one or both partners in the marriage. Also, we may question the events we've seen and those we did not see.

Our next question as an observer of this problem may naturally be how can we help Grandfather? However, if we take a moment to look at the larger war between good and evil, we can recognize that this was a reality for Grandfather—a battle. The question then becomes, "How does God guide us to help Grandfather?"

What can a 12 year-old boy do in the war between God and the Devil? What can any of us do in the daily battles that take place? The Devil attempts to steal joy and happiness from our intimate relationships, while God offers his unconditional love to heal us. We can purposefully and mindfully ask Jesus to guide us to do God's Will. Once we do that, we just need to follow our heart. Are we the persons guided to help Grandfather or not? Is Grandfather ready to see the silver lining? Only God knows.

On our journey to create intimacy with God and others, using Jesus as a vessel, we can be available to carry on God's message. However, we have to be willing to listen to Jesus in our heart to know what to do and say. Perhaps grandfather believed he had been with the love of his life. Maybe he did not need companionship at this stage of his life. Would he find happiness in the future? These are the things you might say to yourself if a loved one died. While we may worry about Grandfather and his view on marriage, we do not need to carry his burden. We can most definitely take confidence that God has a plan for Grandfather's joy as well as ours; God can create the best reality possible for all of us when allow Him access to activate our Volcano Heart.

When something upsetting happens in your life, we may feel a number of different emotions. Feelings are real, and it is healthy for us to recognize how we feel. As you work through what could entail a plethora of feelings, remember to ask God for help. Sometimes we forget this step, and God forgives us for that. Many of us wallow in despair by trying to carry the burden by ourselves. When you are ready, take the first step toward winning back your joy and intimacy in life. You achieve this by praying and asking God to step in and take away the pain. God can show you the silver lining, and God can also make known the way forward through the fog. The people we are blessed to be in a trusting, loving, and intimate relationship with can help us create our best reality. Our faith community, including our priest or pastor and Christian counselors, are available as well whenever God directs us to find help and spiritual healing. When we put our faith and trust in God, He will lead us to redefined intimacy in our lives and our best reality.

Your thoughts, beliefs, and feelings are very real, continuously creating your reality. Your semantics and politics create your life's events, which in turn become your realities. Through your life's ups and downs, your happiness and hardships, and your joy and your pain, you have the opportunity to reset, restart, and redefine yourself and your relationships. Whatever has happened to you has happened. If you have not done so already, now is the time to give your greatest fears, problems, and obstacles to obtaining intimacy to God. He will send Jesus to lessen the load, and bring back the joy and excitement that the Devil has stolen from your Volcano Heart. God will help you redefine your reality to include more intimacy with Him and chosen people in your life, creating more purpose, more meaning, and more satisfaction and joy.

We have discovered how trust and love are necessary to construct intimate relationships. We have also discussed how fear, brought about by the Devil, is a great obstacle to our satisfaction and joy in these relationships. We learned what to do when we experience setbacks in our intimate relationships, and how important it is to stabilize a relationship after a breach of trust or shame from our loved ones about a belief that we have expressed occurs. In the next chapter, we will continue to learn how to mend your broken trust in intimate and meaningful relationships, as well as when to let broken relationships go, with love, that have served their purpose.

You are choosing to live a life of Christian servitude while asking God to increase the intimacy in your life. Your fulfilling future and best reality—a reality full of intimacy, purpose, meaning, and satisfaction—is your goal. Your intimacy, redefined, starts now.

5

Forgiveness

The story of Carl's grandfather congers up a lot of questions. What do you do when a loved one shares a difficult reality? Some of us may want to stay and help, wondering if God has chosen us to help sympathize, reframe the situation, or say something meaningful. Some of us may feel uncomfortable and want to leave thinking to ourselves, "I don't need to be the one to deal with this." Listening to how others have been wronged can shake our reality and belief system, and it can send us into our own negative thought cycle about those who have wronged us. Internalizing something that goes wrong in a relationship, or when we learn about a breach of trust in our own relationship, the greatest question becomes, "How can we forgive those who wrong us?"

Forgiveness of a Past Event

Tonight was the night! Anthony had been waiting for this night for a long time. He donned his handsome new suit with unquestionable pride and confidence, and slipped into his sleek leather shoes. His loving and supportive partner of 20 years was by his side. Anthony had finally decided to face his fears. He was going to go to his 30-year high school reunion. He had finally overcome the painful memories of grade school. He had even forgiven the handful of people who had made him dread his alarm clock every morning.

Anthony had come a long way. But would all of his preparations be enough to face the bullies who had tormented him for so many years? No, he had never been physically harmed. He had never even been publicly humiliated. It was even possible that no one else may have even known, but Anthony knew. He knew not to leave his clothes on the bench in the locker room, or they would go missing. He knew not to walk in front of the bullies, or they would trip him. He also learned to eat his lunch before lunchtime, or it would get taken.

Back then, Anthony had put so much energy into protecting himself at school. He grew to hate these boys for a long time. After about ten years of asking himself "Why me?" he finally had enough separation from the bullies and the wisdom to start asking God, "What for?" He understood that when things happen, good or bad, we all make choices. The higher road is forgiveness. Forgiveness is not the same as forgetting or saying we are ok with what happened to us. When we forgive, we are saying, "God, I give this situation to you. This happened, and I didn't like it. Please heal me and everyone involved." Anthony took himself out of the situation—he was safe now. Now God had given him the wisdom and understanding to forgive.

Can you relate to this story of grade school survival? At different times in your life, have you played different roles? Which role can you identify with—survivor, bystander, bully? When you hear stories like this, you may ask yourself, "What's the big deal? What is the worst that could have happened? It's not like they killed him." On the surface it appears to be just a power struggle, a show of weakness and strength. "Sticks and stones may break my bones, but words can never hurt me," is the age-old advice that we are given. Maybe you are thinking, "Anthony is too sensitive. He needs to toughen up." Then there are the people who say, "What evidence do you have?" These are all questions that many people may ask, but none are the most important questions. Given that this is Anthony's reality, these are the wrong questions to ask.

Something has happened, this is Anthony's reality, and we need to ask ourselves—what can be done about this? Your feelings are real. We have likely played different roles throughout the stories of our lives. Sometimes you may be the survivor in the story of your life; sometimes you may have played the role of a bully. Other times you may be a bystander, wondering if you should do something or hoping that someone else will have the courage to step in and stop the injustice. What is the Christian thing to do when you or someone else is bullied?

God wants us to be safe. It is not ok if your day revolves around protecting yourself from other people. It is ok to ask for help. Tell God about the situation. By taking this first step with faith in Jesus, you are going to be alright. Ask Him to guide you to someone whom you can trust.

God can tell you what to do and whom to invite into the situation. God may guide you to talk to a trusted professional if you are expending energy to stay away from someone or something. Confess your fears and dreams to the Lord. Trust in the Lord's guidance, and God will bridge the gap between your experienced reality and your desired reality.

Whether you are the one who was being wronged or you were the wrong-doer, we must give the situation to God. Struggles may be a part of life, but what does God want us to do about them? Be honest about the times in your life that you have played these roles.

Now that we have recognized what roles we have played in the past, let us take the next step to forgiveness and ask God to take these situations from us. How do we do it? This is indeed easier said than done. In fact, this could be one of the hardest things you will ever do. This pain can creep up on you everyday until you ask God to take it from you, and you allow Him to heal you.

The Slippery Spouse

"Here we go again," Brendon thought to himself. "Every time we go to one of Angela's office parties, she always seems to disappear with Mark." Mark was one of her male coworkers. Brendon understood the importance of supporting his wife's career. By attending her work functions, he was trying to help Angela make connections for her success. However, after a few hours Brendon would run out of casual things to talk about. He would look around for Angela, only to see her emerge from a dark corner or a private room with her favorite male coworker. "Why does Mark get all her attention?" he would ask himself. Afterwards, Brendon would approach Angela with the same question. She always had an excuse for why she went off with Mark, usually saying they had something work related to talk about. "What could they possibly be talking about?"

Brendon tried to act as if it didn't bother him that Angela no longer tried to connect with him, at parties or even when they were together at home. Brendon had always imagined marriage as a partnership, but Angela often acted like a teenager, running away from her parents to be with her friends. Brendon was really unhappy. He would often ask himself," Why is Angela not friends with me anymore?" He always assumed his spouse would be his best friend, however in his current relationship with Angela, Brendon felt like a kid eating alone in the lunchroom everyday.

Brendon and Angela married 10 years ago. Although he had his doubts about her faithfulness even in the beginning of their relationship, he always passed them off as a lack of his own confidence. After all, Angela always claimed that she was faithful to her relationship with Brendon whenever he expressed his doubts. Now, 10 years later, he could not understand why they hadn't grown out of these problems. "When will I feel like Angela wants to be present in our relationship rather than experiencing this feeling of trying to hold on to my runaway wife?" he thought to himself. Like trying to hold water in his hands, Angela was slippery—she was difficult to hold on to and required too much energy to sustain. He wanted Angela to share the workload of relationship maintenance for a change. Brendon longed to be able to trust Angela's fidelity, and furthermore, he wanted to experience the cathartic friendship he believed used to exist in their relationship.

Brendon and Angela went home after the party, and Brendon questioned Angela about some of her relationships. Angela told Brendon he was crazy for imagining that something more than friendship was going on, but Brendon knew he was not imagining feeling a lack of intimacy. Angela was always so secretive. She had a lot of private jokes with Mark and other guys that Brendon didn't understand. She always hid her phone screen and computer screen when Brendon walked into the room. The guys Angela had relationships with were friends with Angela, but Brendon did not count them as friends of their marriage. Brendon was tired of constantly spending so much energy trying to connect with Angela and become a welcome part of her life. Rather than having meaningful conversations with Brendon, Angela seemed to place a higher value on having meaningful conversations with other people in her life. Brendon was exhausted from constantly worrying and wondering, "When is Angela going to want to be in this marriage?"

Let us think about the Redefined Intimacy Scale as well as the Intimacy Ladder regarding this marriage relationship. It is hard to be in a relationship in which you do not have similar desires for intimacy from each other. Intimacy grows from trust and love. If you are constantly worried about a romantic partner cheating on you, whether emotionally or physically, your relationship can become devoid of trust. When Brendon assesses his redefined intimacy, where do you believe he will rate the intimacy of his marriage? Even if Angela were to assess the intimacy of their marriage as high, her behavior in their relationship of keeping secrets and withholding information, has confined the relationship to a low rung on the Intimacy Ladder. Whether you see this situation from Angela's side or Brendon's side, Angela and Brendon have a mismatched desire for intimacy in their relationship.

We have just read 2 different stories. Brendon's problem with his spouse is ongoing and current. Anthony's childhood bullying requires healing, even as it's a past event. Both Anthony's story and Brendon's story require forgiveness. With a current or ongoing problem, we have another question that must be addressed—how do you heal from a relationship wound that is ongoing and current without taking yourself out of the situation?

Now we have a more difficult life question—what if what needs to be forgiven is still happening in your life? Take a look at relationships in your life that require forgiveness. Now that we are coming to terms with these different situations in our lives, we ask God to step inside our space between what we want to experience and what we are experiencing. Have faith and trust in the Lord. Recognizing what is happening in our reality that we are unhappy with is the first step to forgiveness. This recognition of a wrong that requires forgiveness must be followed by giving it to God if we are to achieve forgiveness. What does God want us to do about wrongs that are currently happening in our life? Who does God guide us to involve as we ask God to rewrite our story?

Relationship Death

People search for control in different ways. What control does Brendon have in this story of mismatched intimacy with Angela? Brendon can only control himself. Brendon cannot control his wife and her choices. You do not necessarily need to experience a separation or divorce to experience the death of a relationship.

How would you feel if you thought your spouse was not interested in connecting with you? If you feel like you are losing a relationship that is mismatched in intimacy, you may find yourself entering the stages of relationship grief. We can look at the stages of grief as defined by Elisabeth Kübler-Ross for death and dying and apply them to a dead or dying relationship (Kromberg). If Brendon and Angela hope to have successful intimacy with each other, both of them must take responsibility to either rekindle the existing relationship or choose to leave this relationship. They may still be married, but Brendon's relationship with Angela is dead. Recognizing the death of a relationship is recognizing a reality, but choosing to grieve and mourn the relationship by asking God for help is progress toward successful forgiveness. Let us use Brendon's story as an example as we look at the stages of grief in relationship death.

Stages of Grief in Relationship Death, based on Kübler-Ross's Five Stages of Grief:

Shock and Denial: "This cannot be happening; I am imagining this. Without real evidence that my spouse is cheating, why would I want to risk everything I have worked for and end the marriage?" Things will get better; this is just a phase.

Anger: "How could God allow me to enter into a marriage like this? This has happened, and I did not like it. I have been wasting my time, energy, and treasure."

Bargaining: "If we just move away from her coworker or she gets another job, we can reestablish our relationship."

Depression or Feeling Hopeless: "All relationships are probably like this. Why should I leave all the hard work I have put into this relationship just to start over in a new one and experience the same problems again?"

Acceptance of the loss of the marriage/relationship: "I will forgive my spouse and I will forgive myself. I trust in God to tell me what to do and whom to talk with about this reality. This relationship is currently dead, and I will take God's lead on whether or not this relationship can be rekindled with redefined intimacy. I am not alone; God loves me. I will mourn the loss of intimacy from this relationship, feeling a deep sense of sorrow for our sins."

If you find that you are in a relationship devoid of intimacy, whether due to a need to forgive or a mismatched intimacy, ask God for help. Let God guide you to others in your faith community who can help you work through these stages of the death of your relationship. As you release the pain and forgiveness to God, He will heal you. When two people experience the death of a relationship, whether or not you will heal together or separately, is a question for God.

With God, miracles are possible. If God guides you to create a new relationship with the same person, He knows you will be starting where you left off—the ground level of the Intimacy Ladder. This level is devoid of trust and stability, which must be rebuilt in order for a healthy relationship to exist. God can help both people in the relationship recognize that they are starting from the bottom with the intention of climbing together and rebuilding. Both of you must forgive yourselves and each other. Both of you must rely on Jesus to help you construct the Intimacy Ladder. By recognizing anchors, and guiding your boats toward deeper intimacy with God, you can bring new life to a dead relationship. However, only God knows if the other person is capable of achieving intimacy with you, so ask God how He wants you to proceed.

Think about a mismatched intimacy in your life. Have you ever experienced the death of a relationship? Have you asked God to heal you from this? How has God helped you overcome this situation? In order to heal from these situations, we must give them to God by offering forgiveness for ourselves and others. As a part of the forgiveness process, we can offer prayers for all involved as we mourn the death of these relationships.

Releasing anger and pain to God in order to achieve forgiveness and healing throughout the story of your life can seem immensely difficult. Indeed it may feel like trying to take a giant leap with no running start. Let us now look at how we can take smaller steps to achieve the larger goal of forgiveness for ourselves and others.

Achieving the State of Forgiveness

"Jesus saith unto him, I say not unto thee, Until seven times; but, Until seventy times seven."

Matthew 18:22, ASV

We know that our willingness to forgive others is actually a requirement for us to receive God's forgiveness. We need to remember that obtaining God's forgiveness is the ultimate goal. That indeed may be the only thing that keeps us focused on achieving forgiveness of others that have wronged us in our lives. While considering whom you need to forgive, also ask yourself from whom you require forgiveness?

Ask yourself, "Do I create peace or chaos?" Creating peace does not mean that you never have a disagreement or that you get along with everyone. However, when peace is in your heart, you may have already discovered that God will keep you sheltered from chaotic situations. If you are in a chaotic situation and you cry out to the Lord for peace, your way forward may become clear.

We can look to the Bible for guidance on forgiveness in the face of life struggles. In the story of Daniel and the Lion's Den in the *Book of Daniel* in the Bible, Daniel is thrown into the Lion's den for worshipping God. How can this be? Daniel was a peaceful person and a good servant to the King. The bullies had come to blame him and found him at fault for breaking a rule. Yes, Daniel had really broken the rule, but how could the Lord allow such a horrible life experience to happen to a righteous and peaceful person like Daniel?

Daniel prayed to the Lord in this time of need, and because of Daniel's faith, God closed the mouth of the Lion so that it could not eat Daniel! In the morning, when the officials opened the door, they were amazed to find Daniel still alive! They released Daniel, and instead threw his accusers into the Lion's Den. This time, God opened the Lion's mouth again, and hungry from a day without food, the lion ate Daniel's accusers.

"Why did Daniel have to live through such a horrible experience?" you may ask? It seems like a punishment. We do not always understand the ways of the Lord, and a life as a devout Christian does not mean a life without challenges and obstacles to overcome. In Daniel's case, the law was changed so that it was no longer illegal for Daniel to pray. How can you relate Daniel's struggle to your own life? Think of the good that has come out of your struggles that you have trusted to God.

When we encounter a struggle or a life difficulty, we may be quick to assign blame to someone. Whether or not we continue our relationship with that person, we must offer forgiveness for this person. Forgiveness of others is necessary to continue to grow our relationship with God. The act of forgiveness only says you agree to give the problem to God, not that you are ok with what has happened.

Right now, ask Jesus to search your heart for the people in your life that you need to forgive. As you picture the people before you, imagine letting them walk away from you in peace, releasing them back to God from your mental prison of anger and hatred. Be sure that if you see yourself in the prison of anger, you let yourself go in peace to God as well. For further reading and a good forgiveness exercise similar to the one above, see *Healing With The Angels* on the suggested readings page of this book.

We often ask ourselves, "Why has this happened to me?" This question is a natural response to a difficult life situation. In order to move past feelings of denial, anger, resentment, depression, and hate, we must move into asking ourselves, "What is the reason for this to happen to me?" Or simply put, "How come?" Ask God to help you process your feelings so you can focus on the life lessons. *"Lord, come. Lord, let me see. Amen."*

Look at your life experiences and relationship struggles. You may find that as soon as you learn the life lesson, your faith in God will save you from your lion's den. Maybe you are currently in a difficult season in your life. No matter what you are going through or what has happened to you, you get to decide what to do next. You get to write the next chapter. Trust God to write the best one yet.

How can we forgive those who wrong us? You cannot control other people, but you can control yourself. Take control of your life by asking God for help with forgiveness of others as well as forgiveness of yourself. Your intimacy with God will deepen with this process, and the potential for your relationships with others will become clear.

6

Trust, Love, Friendship, and Marriage

In that last chapter, we found that a great process to increase the intimacy and satisfaction of our relationships is forgiveness. Forgiveness is the act of letting go of a wrong and giving it to God. It does not mean that you agree with what has taken place, it only means that you give it to God to be healed. While forgiveness of others is a part of our Christian servitude, the act of forgiveness does not necessarily return your trust to the relationship, nor does it guarantee the life of a relationship. In fact, when we lose trust in a relationship and forgiveness is required, we can only rely on God to tell us if and when it is safe to restore our trust in a relationship. In your intimate relationships that survive the test of time, give glory to God, for He has been your guide. Let us look at the subject of trust with a story about two co-workers, and a dispute about where an idea originated.

The Stolen Idea at Work

Emelda was so angry, she wanted to throw her computer out of the window! She was cursing herself for not creating and maintaining a record of the development of her project. She had no proof that it was her idea! Did her co-worker, Jack, really think this idea was his, or did he steal the idea on purpose? Before she went to their boss, she wanted to talk to Jack about it, but she wasn't even sure he knew right from wrong. Three weeks into production, Emelda got up the courage to talk to Jack about it. She had all the information she needed. She had the timeline of events that she had piecemealed together. She had the scribbles on post it notes, and a printout of the messages on her phone. Emelda went into her appointment with Jack. She laid everything out for him. She showed him all the evidence that the idea was hers.

What do you suspect happened next? What we suspect happened next in the story of Emelda and Jack can be greatly influenced by our past experiences in life. Our willingness, or unwillingness, to trust other people can greatly affect how we see current events. Has something like this ever happened to you? Truth is a relative concept. Even if this has happened to Emelda in the past, it does not mean that it is also happening now. Emelda has her suspicions, however, Emelda made an appointment with her co-worker to help her determine if her suspicions are correct. She is trying to resolve this problem from a position of a willingness to learn instead of already knowing.

Here are some possible outcomes to Emelda's meeting with Jack:

1. Admission of Guilt/Confession—"I'm so sorry. It will never happen again. Let's make it right."

2. The Perpetual Lie—A denial of guilt, but you know the truth. You recognize an existing pattern of dissatisfaction in the relationship due to lack of trust.
3. A Misunderstanding and Proper Credit Given—"I put your name on the inventor list and gave the team credit where credit was due."
4. An Honest Misunderstanding/Co-Evolution—There was a co-creation of an idea where there is proof that it was genuinely Jack's idea as well.

When we take action to resolve a grievance in our life situations, we can get carried away with the series of events—the politics and the meanings behind them. Looking at the relationship between Jack and Emelda, and Emelda's grievance toward Jack, what would God want you to do in each of these possible outcomes? Emelda is not only thinking of salvaging her credit for her idea. She is also taking this grievance a step further and wondering if she should remain friends with Jack. In order to know the answer of how we can ensure we are in a trusting relationship, we need to remember to invite God into the situation. In any given grievance or situation that requires forgiveness, we have three choices. We can choose to leave the relationship, stay in the relationship, or wait and see what will happen. God can direct us to make the right choices.

What will happen between Jack and Emelda? Will they remain friends? Based on what is determined to have happened by Emelda, and whether or not Emelda can restore the trust in this relationship will determine the answer. Many things may take place in the story of Jack and Emelda. Regardless of the future status of their friendship, Emelda has another important choice to make. Will Emelda choose to forgive or will she choose to be resentful?

Remember from the previous chapter, forgiving means recognizing something happened and choosing to give the situation to God to be healed. Forgiveness does not dictate the action of staying or leaving, and it does not restore trust in a relationship. Only God can be relied on to restore trust. Staying, leaving, and waiting to see, are all possible actions we can take. As we let God into the everyday experiences of our lives, He can guide us what to do when we experience a lack of trust. There is no right or wrong answer. There is only what we choose to do. However, in relationships, it is more than just you. In any relationship—at work with co-workers and managers, at home with family or roommates, and with friendships—there are other people involved.

What rung on the Intimacy Ladder would you place a coworker who steals your ideas? The act of stealing creates a lack of trust, which in turn creates a mismatch in intimacy. Since the level of intimacy in a relationship is determined by the lowest level, your relationship with someone who you believe has stolen something from you is in fact at a level one—no common ground, no trust. To determine if a relationship can be repaired is to determine if you desire to stay in the relationship that was damaged. The question becomes, "Is this a relationship I want or need to maintain?"

Ideally, we would not enter into or stay in any relationship that is at a level one in intimacy on the grounds that it is unhealthy. The reality of working with someone you do not trust is challenging. How unfulfilling would that relationship be? Even with forgiveness being obtained, there must be trust in order to progress to the next level of intimacy in this friendship. What is the ideal level of intimacy you would like to see in your relationships with people you see every day—the people that you work or live with?

Love and Marriage

Life is so much more than your career, your family, and your friends. As Christians, our purpose in life is to live for God. "Life on earth is work, and the vacation happens when we are in heaven (Goddard)." At the beginning of this book, you learned about increasing your intimacy with God and therefore redefining intimacy in your life. For intimacy in your marriage, you must also make a choice to grow your intimacy.

Before we enter into a marriage, we may ask ourselves many questions. *How do we trust that we are with the person God wants us to marry? There are so many potential life partners, how could we possibly choose? How do we know if God wants us to stay or leave a marriage? What level of intimacy do you expect to experience with your spouse? When does this intimacy get established?* These are just some of the many important questions people ask themselves before asking the most important question, "Should I spend my life with this person?"

Thinking about spending the rest of your life with someone can be both exciting and overwhelming. Let us look at love in terms of intensity. God loves us the most of all—unconditionally; a ten on the top of the Intimacy Ladder. That means no matter what we do and say, God Will still love us, and He will still be interested in continuing our relationship. God's love is unchanging. This does not mean that God does not challenge us, forming us into better people. If you were to take God's love and intimacy, and use it as an example for your marriage and all the relationships of your lifetime, what would they look like?

What does it look like to try to love your spouse with unconditional love? As we are not God, we are not perfect. Remember, unconditional love is a much higher intimacy and cognitive state than we may ever hope to obtain. You should not mistake this ideal as a reason to stay in an unhealthy relationship. Sometimes, even unconditional love requires you to love a person so much that you allow them to grow on their own and without you. When you discover an intimacy mismatch in any area of your life, remember that your intimacy with God remains. The best way we can honor our marriage relationship is to ask Jesus to try to take us to the highest level of intimacy, and see where He leads us.

It's difficult to talk about marriage without also thinking about divorce. If someone mentions being unhappy in a marriage, experiencing trials and obstacles or loneliness, people are quick to jump to their own belief system about what should be done and what steps to take. Whether or not you believe in divorce or separations as a solution, you should respect that God intends for you to live a life of love in a trusting relationship. God is all-knowing and everywhere. If we trust God with our marital problems, He will make the solution known. If you feel alone, unloved, or unsafe, those feelings are real. They are also robbing you of intimacy in your life. Take the first step, and ask God to tell you what to do. As you pray, pour out your heart and ask God to send Jesus to save you from your feelings of isolation. Listen to His answer. God will guide you within your faith community to an answer that is better than anything you can imagine, and the best outcome for all involved. We do not always understand the, "Why me?" and the "How come?" But, with God we can always trust His love for us will lead us to a resolution. Whether that resolution is expected or unexpected, the challenge is asking God for help and then listening to His answer.

Achieving Successful Intimacy in Relationships

What is the reason you stay in a relationship when something difficult happens, that you need to forgive and restore trust? Whether the relationship is a friendship, a marriage or another familial relationship, the answer can be complicated and needs to evolve between you and God. Resources to help with life-changing choices can be your priest or pastor, your Christian counselor, and others to whom God guides you to seek advice.

Why choose a priest or counselor rather than a friend or family member? These people are likely to be free of bias, compared to someone in your life who may be affected by your decision to make a change. For example, let's say you are contemplating a divorce and you want to ask a friend or family member for advice. This may be a good choice for some people. However, if this friend or family member is in your life, they will likely be affected by how your decision will effect them. It also places a heavy burden on the friend or family member who may worry about you. Whoever God guides you to seek advice from, remember that you are not alone. Although this relationship decision may be very difficult, you can rewrite your reality with God. Start the conversation with God. You can simply say, "God, what should I do now, and whom do you guide me to talk to about this?"

Choose to take the step to building redefined intimacy in your life by asking, "Lord, what should I do in my existing intimate relationships, and with whom should I build a relationship?" We can choose to ask God for guidance everyday and in every relationship. God can bring healthy intimacy into your relationships and your life to free you from feelings of isolation, betrayal, and lack of control. For any relationship where trust has been broken, we can have faith that Jesus will either restore our trust and heal the relationship, or steer us away from the relationship. We need only to ask God for guidance, and follow His advice.

Achieving successful intimacy in relationships requires a desire to grow intimacy, trust, and love through God. What relationships in your life possess trust and higher love? Let God guide you in your relationships. Allow God into every relationship and watch your life transform as your intimacy is redefined. Remember, not everyone is on the same journey. Even those on the same journey may be anchored in an important stage of their personal intimacy journey.

At times, God may call you to help someone else in a nearby boat on your journey. You can choose to listen to and respect these other people as a part of your divine assignment from God. By continually choosing to live a life of Christian servitude, you can create union, and even friendship, with people God guides you to help.

Let your heart be as free-flowing as the wind with Christian servitude as your direction. When you go where God takes you, it is always the correct direction. Speaking of going the right direction, it feels great to go where like-minded people are interested in creating positive and meaningful relationships. Ask for God to find like-minded people for you, who can grow together in this life. Together with God, you can create opportunities for redefined intimacy. Who are these people you will meet?

These are people who are on the journey with you. Their age, race, and their nationality should not matter. Their social status, career, and their family relationship should not matter. Even their religious and spiritual beliefs should not matter. As long as God guides you to increase redefined intimacy with another person, you are on the right track.

God can bring you into opportunities to experience loving and trusting relationships that can evolve into friendships or a marriage. God can steer you away from toxic, harmful, and mismatched relationships. Loving, Christ-centered relationships—full of trust and love—can be the basis of friendships and marriage relationships. A community of believers on the same journey as you are out there. Ask God to help you find each other. Ask God to help you find your people.

Psalm 39:7 ASV

"And now, Lord, what wait I for? My hope is in thee."

7

Terms of Commitment

You can feel strong now in Christ as you read along and think of how these things have affected your relationships on your personal journey to redefine intimacy in your life. Think back to the beginning of your journey towards increasing intimacy with God—what about the people that chose to stay on the docks? Are we going back to get them? Some of them are your family and your friends. Do you feel like you have left someone behind? You may desire to share things you have learned with them. You want to bring them with you to experience the same joy that you have found! You just know they will appreciate it as you have. Take a moment now to align your heart with Jesus. What does your heart say? What does your Christ-centered heart tell you to do about each one of the family and friends that are on a different journey? It's possible that some of your loved ones are on a life journey that has them anchored far away from you.

Let us reassess the terms of our commitment to redefined intimacy in our lives. Consider these three possible outcomes to developing intimacy in your relationships on your journey to redefine intimacy in your life:

Terms of Commitment on Your Journey to Redefined Intimacy with God and Others

- **Enjoy your Friendship**—Equally support each other on the same journey.
- **Divine Assignment**—You can help them, allowing Jesus to provide you energy for this task.
- **Respect the Chosen Path of Others**—Follow God's guidance to allow others the opportunity to help this person.

Remember God loves us all unconditionally. Only God sees the big picture. If you contest God's decision, either thinking you are doing a goodwill or simply because your listening was turned off, you will be going against God's Will. What does it mean to go against God's Will? It is a common temptation that we all experience on our journey to get to know God. God forgives us for our struggle to do the right thing as we zigzag, swerve, or even when we veer away from His will. God looks forward to us getting back on His journey for us.

We can control what we do, but not what others do. Let us talk about the control we have in a situation when a loved one has decided to stay on the dock, jump in without a boat, or go in a different direction. You can use the following "Three Step Discernment Exercise for Helping Others", to help you determine what to do next in your relationships.

Three Step Discernment Exercise for Helping Others

1. **Tell God About Your Concerns**—Pray, ask for guidance from Jesus.
2. **Listen**—God answers your prayers. Follow through with what God tells you to do.

3. **Choose God's Will**—Make the choice to constantly align with God's Will.

One of the best realizations as a Christian is that, with Jesus in your heart, you are not responsible for others or their choices. Is that not a completely freeing thought? We can only control ourselves. We cannot control other people. God has a plan for everyone.

Recall these statements from Chapter One and let us see if they now have a more intimate meaning: "If we do not develop an intimacy with God, we have nothing in this life. No matter how many friends and family we have, no matter how much wealth and health we have, we have nothing if we do not have quality, meaningful, and intimate relationships that are based on the word of God and our life purpose. God gives us everything we need to fulfill our purpose." Now ask God to help you with your family member or friend. "God, are you calling me to help them?" The answer is between you and Jesus. Feel your intimacy with Jesus grow deeper and deeper as you allow the Lord complete control of the answer. Heed His response and let God's will unfold.

Every day is filled with opportunities to deepen your intimacy with the Lord. Try it! Develop your own personal way of talking to and interacting with God. Are you committed to allowing Jesus in your life to strengthen your intimacy with God, and all the relationships in your life? Let's talk about tools that God gives us to grow these relationships with intimacy.

One of these tools is discernment. Let's look at situations we encounter in our lives, and what they mean for us on our Christian journey toward developing intimacy with God and people in our lives. We can use discernment in the following situation and then practice using it with an example from our own life.

Imagine you have an invitation for a new experience in your life. Let's say you have an interview about a subject you are very knowledgeable about, and the opportunity to meet and make a new friend. How does your decision to accept or turn down the invitation affect your Christian journey of creating more meaningful relationships? In order to answer this question, you can ask God to help you discern what is important and what is not important on your life's journey. When should you spend your energy on a project, and when should you direct your energy elsewhere? Remember, using discernment is different from making a judgment.

Increase your intimacy with God with this discernment exercise. This example involves switching jobs to determine if your life choice is in alignment with God's Will and your best reality possible.

Discernment Exercise for a Life Event

1. **Determine the Question You Have for God**—"Dear God, should I switch jobs?"
2. **Assess Your Values, Needs, and Desires**—"I would really like a job where I make good money, have reliable coworkers that I can have a relationship with, and have a boss who respects me and understands my job."
3. **Be Honest About Your Fears, Worries, and Misgivings**—"I'm worried that if I change jobs, I won't have anything in common with the people who work there and I'm too tired to learn a new skill."

4. **Listen to God's Answer**—God always answers us. Sometimes the answer might surprise us. God's answer is always a blessing for all people involved.

Using discernment in your daily life can help you maintain the meaningfulness in your relationships while forging new intimacy relationships and opportunities. Try the discernment exercise with something you have been meaning to ask the Lord.

Reassessing your life choices can help keep you in tune with God, thereby increasing the intimacy and meaningfulness in your life. What can you do to help you assess your life? The process of life assessment and reassessment is a healthy habit. It may seem like a lofty goal, but we can create smaller, easy to accomplish habits that will ultimately lead us to the overall goal of spending more time with the Lord. Consider creating healthy habits as a tool for getting closer to the Lord. With the goal of getting closer to God by inviting God to help us with discerning life situations, here are a few of my favorite choices for spending time with God.

Healthy Habits for Spending Time With God

1. **Meditate**—Try starting with 2 or 3 minutes a day. Set your calendar to remind yourself. Clear your head and be still, inviting God into your heart and mind.
2. **Yoga/Tai Chi/Chi Kung**—The practice of Yoga can create harmony in the mind, body, and spirit. The rhythmic movements of Tai Chi and Chi Kung can move energy through your body, thus helping to stimulate the spiritual, mental, and physical body.
3. **Walking or Aerobics**—Many people find they have the best ideas after physical activity. Try walking or aerobics for at least 10 minutes each day to connect with the Lord.

4. **Prayer**—Create a prayer routine. Common times are in the morning, at meal times, and before bed. Any time is the right time to pray.
5. **Reading the Bible**—Try a few verses each night before bed. You can download a Bible app to your phone, and the app will allow you to choose how often you receive a Bible verse notification. Are you feeling up for a challenge? Try one of the many Bible programs that has reading assignments for each day of the year. You can start a daily Bible reading program on any day of the year, but the goal is to create the habit of reading some of the Bible each day. At the end of one year, you will have completed reading the entire Bible.
6. **Church Services**—These can help you create the habit of spending one hour a week devoted to the Lord. People coming together in worship is a time-honored tradition for good reason.
7. **Religious Education and Religious Discussions**—Podcasts and Bible Studies of your choice are available everywhere.
8. **Friends and Family**—Have meaningful discussions about God and your life journey with others that have chosen a redefined intimacy in their lives.
9. **Religious Groups/Volunteer Groups**—Coming together for the Glory of God is a powerful thing. Learn about God in a group where other people are interested in learning about God as well.
10. **Religious Retreat or Mission**—Sometimes taking yourself out of your daily routine and spending time in a peaceful, motivational setting is just the thing to

jumpstart a new healthy habit. This time away can allow you to reassess where you are with God's Plan for you.

How are you doing on your journey to increase your intimacy with God and others in your life? Have you tried any of these methods to increase your intimacy with God? Almost any activity you can think of can increase your intimacy with God, as long as that is your intention. As you continue to increase your intimacy with God, He will continue to guide you how to increase your intimacy with others on your life journey. Try using the discernment exercise, and see which of the ten suggested healthy habits work best for you to increase the redefined intimacy in your relationships. The union that can develop from sharing your beliefs is a satisfying and fulfilling redefined intimacy that I pray you obtain with your loved ones.

8

Prayer

Prayer is the most important aspect of Christian life. Prayer is a tool that can bring us closer to God on our journey of redefined intimacy. Through prayer, we recognize that God is the Creator of heaven and earth, both the Father and the Son, and the bringer of the Holy Spirit. Every time we perform the sign of the Cross—God the Father, God the Son, and God the Holy Spirit—we recognize God as the Holy Trinity. As we develop our intimacy with the Lord God, there is one prayer that remains paramount—*The Lord's Prayer*.

The Lord's Prayer

"Our Father, who art in Heaven, hallowed be thy name. Thy Kingdom Come, Thy Will be done, on Earth as it is in Heaven. Give us this day, our daily bread and forgive us our trespasses as we forgive those who trespass against us. And lead us not into temptation, but deliver us from evil. Amen."

In the Bible, Jesus is asked how to pray. He responds with the "Our Father," also known as the Lord's Prayer. The prayer recognizes that God is Holy, prays for God's Will to be done, and asks for wisdom and understanding. The prayer also asks for forgiveness of us as we are all sinners, while offering that we will in turn forgive others who do us wrong. Just as our Father God forgives us, we must forgive other people.

We have been talking about offering prayer to God at times of need or discernment. When we need something, we are most likely aware of it. These times of need are opportunities when we can learn to reach out to God through Jesus. We may pray for a solution to a problem, or for the removal of an obstacle keeping us from what we need or want. We may pray for guidance in taking an important life step, help making a decision, or we may ask for discernment in our lives. We can develop our own way of talking to God as well as our own prayers. This effort can help bring us into a state of readiness for sending and receiving intimacy with God. Here are some of my favorite prayers for talking to God.

Morning Prayer (developed after I read, *A Course in Miracles, by Helen Schucman*)

Dear God in the name of Jesus,

Please help us today. We pray that Jesus comes to forgive us our sins and atone us. We pray that everything we do, we do for God's Will and in God's name, and we ask, "What miracles can we preform for you today?" We pray that God, Jesus, and Mary send love into our hearts, so we can all go out and be shining examples of your light. We pray that we are protected from being ensnared by the devil. We pray for our nation and for all the nations of the world. We pray for ourselves, our friends, our families, and even our enemies, that we all receive the gifts of the Spirit and God's blessings in accordance with God's Will.

In Jesus name we pray, Amen.

Prayer for Health and Healing

Dear God in the name of Jesus,

Thank you for complete health and healing. If my illness/ailment has served its purpose, please let it pass quickly. I have faith that you will heal me and lead me to perfect health. Should I need a provider and care, please lead me where to receive help. I pray that I am free of pain and full of life and energy until I complete my life purpose here on earth. Amen.

Prayer for a Lost Pet

Dear God in the name of Jesus,

Please send Jesus to find my pet. If my pet has passed on, I thank you for our time together. Amen

Prayer for Sleep

Dear God in the name of Jesus,

I pray that I sleep a deep, peaceful, and sound sleep tonight. I pray that my body and mind recover and heal during this sleep and that I awake in the morning feeling refreshed and ready for the day. Amen.

Prayer for Financial Stability and Wealth

Dear God in the name of Jesus,

Please help me discern my finances. Please help me to provide for myself and my family, repay my debts, allow for savings, and help me to reach out to the poor. Please let me be free of the fears of losing money, so that I can live a happy and sound life knowing that you are protecting me financially. Amen.

Prayer to Ease Worries and Fears

Dear God in the name of Jesus,

Please take away the burden of worrying about things that I have no control over. Please take away fears that are ego-based or creating obstacles to my peace and happiness. Let me hear your discernments to guide me safely on my journey rather than this fear and worry. Amen.

Grace Before Meals

Bless us, O Lord and these thy gifts, which we are about to receive, from thy bounty, through Christ Our Lord. Amen.

Prayer for Releasing Guilt and Sin

Dear God,

I am so sorry for (name the sin). Please guide me to do the right thing and not do this again. I want to do good for you. Amen.

Prayer for Friends

Dear God,

Please guide me to deep and meaningful friendships in the name of Jesus. Please allow me the opportunity to experience joy and satisfaction with like-minded people of similar interests. Amen.

Prayer for Soul Mate/ Life Partner

Dear God in the name of Jesus,

Please make me into the best version of myself so that I am ready to receive my soul-mate, or the person you feel is best to share my life events. When we are both ready to be in a loving, committed relationship, please allow us to meet and know that we are meant for each other. Amen.

These are some of my favorite prayers. Any prayer you say, either aloud or to yourself, can increase your intimacy with God. Do you have a favorite prayer?

As we actively lay all of our burdens on Jesus to carry for us through our prayers to God, we may realize that there is more than just our worries and fears. There are good things that we want to share with God! There is more than one type of prayer.

I am talking about gratitude, glory, and blessings. Blessings are wonderful things given to us by God, and we can thank Him for them with gratitude and glory. Would you thank a friend for buying you dinner? Saying thank you is polite, but gratitude is both saying thank you and feeling thankful. **Gratitude** is one of the highest forms of love that we can ever offer. Gratitude is a special tool for building intimacy with God. What a gift to feel the love of our blessings and remembering to share that feeling with God! Here is a gratitude prayer I started saying at night before going to bed.

Gratitude Prayer

Dear God,

Thank you for this day. Thank you for providing us food, water, clothing, and a safe place to live. Thank you for giving (name yourself and your loved ones) steady jobs, and letting us all have a good education. Thank you for letting us live on this earth, and thank you for creating us. Thank you for protecting us from everything and everyone that might hurt us. In Jesus name we pray, Amen.

Do you have a favorite prayer? Maybe you have already developed your own prayers, or ways of talking to God. Perhaps you prefer to sing your prayers, with your favorite hymn or song, to glorify God. The practice of saying or singing prayers on a daily basis—adding prayer as a healthful habit—can increase the frequency of opportunities to build intimacy with God. Growing your relationship with God can bring meaning, purpose, and satisfaction into your life. If you do not know what prayer you want to say, you can always think about your needs or what you are trying to share with God, and then recite *The Lord's Prayer*, which the Bible tells us is the perfect prayer.

When is it appropriate to give glory to God? Always and whenever possible! God utilizes us in different ways. When we become His children and learn to listen to Him, we gain wisdom and understanding of His bigger picture. What a wonderful way to bring meaning into your life through this intimate relationship with the Lord!

9

Community

Congratulations! You have worked through some difficult intimacy realities while reading this book. You are strengthening your relationship with God, and that is always fruitful progress. Are you ready to meet and discover new people and new places that God guides you to discover? Being an active member in a community is another valuable intimacy tool. Open your heart to receive a community of people who are drawn to you as you send redefined intimacy their way. On your journey to redefine the intimacy in your life, others are allowed to come to you because you asked God to bring them to you. You are an important part of God's plan! God gives you everything you need to fulfill your life mission to serve Him. You can experience the redefined intimacy of having God and other loved ones in your life within a loving community based on Christian servitude!

Having everything you need and serving God, even with the support of a loving Christian community, does not mean that you will not be tempted to veer off track. On the contrary, you may find that you will be tested more and more in your life. Use your trials in life as yet another tool to hone your intentions for redefined intimacy with God and others. The wisdom and understanding you gain from Jesus, through life lessons or during anchored seasons of your life, will lead you to blessings. Worry not; you are loved by God unconditionally. You are striving to live a heart-centered life with the intention to please God.

What do others in your community look like? People of different colors, different nations, even different religions. Who are we to judge whom Jesus guides us to befriend or help along their journey? One thing is for certain, as your relationship with the Lord grows in intimacy, you will all be working to have the same Volcano Heart. The heart of Jesus will be alive within you, no matter who you are or what you look like on the outside.

It is natural to experience fears as you set out to open your heart to meet new people to whom God guides you. What if you make a mistake? A wrong choice? What if you hurt someone in your community; your new family? We are all sinners, and as humans we all make mistakes. The difference with having the heart of Jesus is that we intend to come to God with those wrongs in order to trust Him to make them right. Oftentimes when we make a mistake, we will be amazed to watch God heal the situation. That is the very definition of a miracle, and yes, we are worth it! Recognizing our sins, wrongdoings, and mistakes are all opportunities to increase intimacy with God. Allow God to clear your heart, preparing you to give and receive intimacy with others.

There are many religions practiced in the world today. I grew up in the Catholic community. As a practicing Catholic, we learn we can come to a priest with our wrongdoings and ask for God's forgiveness. This is done through the act of confession, and with our prayer for confession. After we confess our sins, we say a prayer known as the *Act of Contrition*, stating our intentions to do better.

Act of Contrition

"My God, I am sorry for my sins with all my heart. In choosing to do wrong and failing to do good I have sinned against you, whom I should love above all things. I firmly intend, with your help, to do penance, to sin no more, and to avoid whatever leads me to sin. Our Savior Jesus Christ suffered and died for us. In his name, my God, have Mercy. Amen." (Rite of penance No. 45)

This prayer serves as a reminder of who we are and our intention to serve Christ. Are you searching for others on a similar journey to share your redefined intimacy? Maybe you are thinking, "I haven't found my people yet." Fear not! First and foremost, continue to work on your relationship with God. Go up the Intimacy Ladder with God, rung by rung. Intimate relationships require time, trust, and maintenance. Let's explore some of the healthy habits we discussed in the previous chapter. We can utilize these habits to work on our relationship with Christ.

Sometimes when you meet a new neighbor, you go over to their house to welcome them to the neighborhood. You give them your phone number, or offer that they come over to your house. Maybe you even bring them a meal or some cookies in an effort to make them feel welcome. Perhaps you have been on the receiving end of these welcoming acts as the new neighbor on the block or in the building. How does it feel to be welcomed? Jesus would like to feel welcomed into our homes and into our hearts. Welcoming Jesus is how we get closer to God. Take this moment to invite Jesus into your heart.

When was the last time you went over to the Lord's house to welcome Him into your home and your heart? I am talking about a Holy place of worship where the Lord resides—the church. Perhaps it has been a while since you have visited your church, or maybe you have not found the right intimacy match for you yet. If it has been a while since you have visited the House of God, consider going in and offering Him a prayer.

No matter what Christian church you belong to, there is a celebration at church at least once a week—a service, or a mass. Attending this service is another tool for building intimacy with God. Everyone is invited to this celebration of life and strength through the Lord. Each religion has different guidelines, but all churches will welcome you. Take the time to look into what the different schools of thought and beliefs are, and see which school of thought is best for you on your journey of redefined intimacy with the Lord. All Christian religions have at least one thing in common—Christians believe that Jesus Christ is our Lord and Savior. Choosing to attend the church service is choosing to celebrate life through Jesus Christ.

What if you are new to a church or you have never attended a service or mass? What better way to learn than to find the person in charge and have them teach you what to do at the House of the Lord! Consider this—if God guides you to go to a church, introduce yourself to the religious minister, pastor, or presiding priest. Let them know if you have been there before, and tell them you are there to grow your relationship with God. A religious leader's life purpose is to help guide us on our life's journey to God. They can become both your teacher and your friend on your journey to redefine intimacy in your life.

Religious establishments usually have services at least once a week, and many also offer religious education—Bible studies. Studying the Bible is another tool for building intimacy with God. The Bible was written in a different time and translated into English and other languages used today. Bible studies are often written by people who have studied the Bible extensively, and people who have been divinely inspired by God. What better way to understand the Books in the Bible than to be taught by someone inspired to facilitate a discussion that will help you increase intimacy with the Lord? As with any learning experience, how can you learn unless you try? Another benefit of getting closer to God at a Bible study is that other people there are also trying to get closer to God. This can be a great way to meet members of your community that already have something in common with you.

Are you feeling reluctant about visiting a church community for a worship service or a Bible study? It is alright to try several different churches to find the right fit for you. As you visit different church services, try to focus on discerning which church is best for you on your redefined intimacy journey. If you are still apprehensive about choosing a church to attend, try focusing on finding a community that is focused on the love of Jesus. When a community is built on the love of Jesus, you can feel it. If God guides you to attend a church, this is a great opportunity to grow your faith and intimacy with the Lord based on the needs of your life journey and potentially the journey of others. Church is a great place to find others at a similar place on the journey of redefined intimacy.

Where are you on your journey to redefine intimacy in your life? The answer to this question requires some insight on your part. We all experience different seasons in our life. You may currently be in a busy season of your life, and you may not have enough energy to join a faith community at this time. In times like these, the most basic thing you can do is focus on prayer. Even something as simple as, "Thank you God for this food," is a prayer. It is an offer of gratitude to God as you feel the words you pray in your heart. When you are ready to grow your gratitude for God by attending the religious celebration of your choice, trust that God will grow the desire in your heart. Your desire to spend more time with the Lord and in different ways may grow as you continue to increase your redefined intimacy with God and his only begotten Son, Jesus Christ. Here is a prayer for finding a church community that is right for you.

Prayer for Finding a Faith Community

Dear God,

Please lead me to a religious school of thought that will bring me closer to you. Help me find the best church to cultivate my relationship with you and others in my life.

Amen.

When you begin to form the habit of prayer, you may feel alone, but you are never alone when you invite God into your life. Is there a prayer that you can add to your life right now? As we add new prayers, new people, and new healthy habits based on our redefined intimacy, we start to develop an excitement! We begin to live and witness our new reality. You may say to yourself, "I can do anything in Christ!" This is a good feeling to have, but it is still important to listen to the guidance of Christ in your heart. God will always answer us, but we must learn to listen to Him. It is important to walk with God, not run ahead of Him. In the seasons of life that we choose to walk with God, we experience God's perfect timing for everything we need.

As we refocus our life to helping other people discover the joy and satisfaction that come from increasing our intimate relationship with God, we need to be wary about running ahead and leaving God behind—something we can refer to as Hero Syndrome. In the next chapter, we will explore the dangers of trying to become a hero to the world. We should always remember that Jesus is the Savior of the World. Keeping Jesus in our heart on every step of our journey ensures that we follow God's Will, and not a will of our own.

10

Best Version of Self for Redefined Intimacy

As we assess our relationships on the pursuit of redefined intimacy in our lives, we can understand the importance of developing the best version of ourselves. In order to establish and grow intimacy, we need to remain open-hearted for the purpose of sending and receiving intimacy. We must be mentally vigorous in order to pursue, experience, and maintain healthy, positive intimacies in our life. If you are going through something in your life right now that is getting in the way of your intimacy with other people, reach out to a professional to whom God guides you. There are so many ways to receive help. While my preference is for a Christian counselor, you may find that God guides you to another type of professional to best suit your needs. If anger, sadness, depression, anxiety, or anything else that is stealing your joy has become overwhelming in your life, now is the right time to seek help and become the best version of yourself. You only have one life. Ask God to help you live the best reality possible, by recognizing your need for help and seeking help when you need it.

Prayer for Receiving Help

Dear God in the name of Jesus,

I am feeling overwhelmed with this (name the problem or feeling). I know you are all-knowing and already know this about me, but as I humble myself, I ask for your help. Please let me know what to do, where to go, and who to talk to about this problem.

Amen.

Hero Syndrome and Savior Complex

With all this talk about the power we have to change our relationships for the better and how to become the best version of you for God, yourself, and for your relationships, it's hard not to become overly excited about our newfound purpose. Be aware of the Volcano Heart laying new ground. God will lay your new ground in the right place and at the right time. This is not an excuse to take hold of that power and attempt to waylay anyone in opposition, flooding their reality with the lava from your Volcano Heart. There is a fine line between standing up for what you believe in, and encroaching on someone else's beliefs and liberties.

What is a hero? Heroes are typically fund in stories or fairytales. Fairytales are stories that involve people faced with challenges. The characters in the fairytales are usually neatly classified as either heroes, villains, or people who suffer from making the wrong and usually selfish decision. The fairytale usually has a happy ending to the struggles and turmoils that were experienced in the story.

Real life is very different from fairytales. Real life is made up of choices, and those choices tell our own story. If we don't like our story, we can ask God to rewrite it. However, in our real life we never get to the end. In essence, your life is not over until you die. Therefore, how do you continue to keep being the good guy and keep making the right choices? On top of that difficulty, some people suffer from what has come to be known in the media as **hero syndrome** or **savior complex**—a belief, absent of God, in which you believe you are responsible for saving everyone who crosses your path; this is the opposite of Christian servitude.

We have talked about discernment—when to stay, when to help, and when to walk away. As you become stronger in your faith relationship with God, it may be hard at times to discern whether you should walk away from something that is contradictory to your beliefs or stand up for your beliefs. For example, you may hear someone else express a belief that is negative or derogatory in nature about something or someone you feel strongly about. Do you say something to defend your belief or walk away? What any of us do or do not do, and say or do not say in these definitive moments may weigh on our minds for years or even decades. The weight of this guilt comes from the feeling that we did something wrong, or out of step with God. Can you think of a time when you were in a dilemma or a confrontation, and you forgot to ask God for help? Tell God about it now.

Adopting God's Will may be different from being a hero to the world. God gave us free will for a reason. We have the right to think, feel, and be however we want. You have free will, just like everyone else. You have to choose to ask for God's help, "God's Will be done," in order to override your free will and adopt God's Will. This choice is one of many ways God shows us his unconditional love.

When insightfully defining ourself in order to be the best version of self for our relationships and our relationship with God, we can focus on hearing and feeling God's unconditional love; positive messages from God. As we discover who we are and who we are not on our life journey, we realize God created a diverse world. Being different promotes many things, including problem solving and finding solutions for better ways of living. We create union with other by focusing on how we are alike, rather than how are we different. Talk to God as you work on your best version of self for God and for your redefined intimate relationships. God will answer your question, "God what should I do?"

When it comes to helping others to whom God guides us in life struggles, speaking with love is always more receptive than exerting power. In other words, we should allow others to use their own free will to make choices rather than try to force them to think or feel a certain way. Love is the strongest catalyst for bringing others to God's love. Using discernment as you adopt God's Will as your own may involve staying, helping, or walking away from the situation at hand.

You can be the your best version of self as you learn to ask God for help. Listen to God's answer, discerning different life situations in an effort to align with God's Will.

Open Heart, Open Mind

How can we maintain an open heart and an open mind in our intimate relationships? When we are free of emotion and free of bias, we are the best receptors of God's discernment. Likewise, when making decisions in life and in our intimate relationships with our loved ones, the best decisions are made when we are level-headed.

Life can get messy. Friends and family do not always see eye to eye. **Meaningful conversations** are the threading of intimate relationships, yet they can take a turn for the worst when we strive to make a point that is based on divide, rather than unity, or already knowing rather than a willingness to learn. While mending these relationship threads is possible and is a normal part of life, addressing the core of the argument is usually where the maximum growth of intimacy can occur. An argument's core is often about maintenance in the sense of quality of life. Therefore, it is important not to support arguments and criticisms as a form of entertainment. We should remain mindful not to argue for the sake of arguing. Rather, from a perspective of Christian servitude, and as one who strives to uphold the ideals of peace, love, and harmony, how can we progress through divide and remain unscathed? How can we remain on our best behavior during chaotic, mind-tormenting, and heart-wrenching conversations? As meaningful conversations are the threading of intimate relationships, redefined intimacy is the fabric of a meaningful, happy, and satisfied life.

In the Bible, it is said to never go to bed angry. However, sometimes our arguments with loved ones are not things that can be solved in a day. Sometimes we are not in a position to be able to put our anger into words. In times of need, when the distress of an intimate relationships is weighing on your mind, ask God for help. In relationships, we all play a role if we are truly present. Apologize for your role, or lack of taking a role, in the argument. Ask God to take away your anger, and to guide you what to say, what to do, and when to wait and see. If a separation from the relationship is necessary for both of you to heal, ask God to help you take the essential steps to part ways through love in Christ.

Let us open our hearts and minds for God to provide us with a clean slate in our healthy and intimate relationships.

Play Well with Others

Throughout this book we have talked about the role of intimacy in our meaningful relationships and using discernment as we listen to God help guide us. However, intimacy with like-minded people does not mean that you are rude and uncaring to others in the world. In fact, the opposite should be true. Now that we understand what intimacy is, the role it plays in our relationships, and its importance, we should also respect other people that we come into contact with in the absence of intimacy. How do we adopt a practice of being a more meaningful and better people while becoming the best version of ourselves?

What if God is guiding you to help someone on your journey for redefined intimacy? By remaining open to receiving messages from God, you are choosing to focus on carrying out God's Will rather than your own. In the absence of friendship or intimacy, you can choose to get along with other people that God guides you to on your journey through **union.** The coming together for a common purpose of carrying out God's Will rather than your own free will. If a union is no longer possible, God will give you the ability to discern what to do next. We can take the following steps on our pathway to maintain the best version of self.

Pathway to Best Version of Self for Redefined Intimacy

1. **Follow God's Will, Not Your Own**—Follow God's Will to experience a more meaningful and purposeful life
2. **Choose to Live a Life of Christian Servitude**— Make the choice to serve God, thereby experiencing a life full of redefined intimacy. Allow God to connect you to

other people with whom God guides you to form intimate relationships.
3. **Focus on Positivity and Union**—Promote peace, harmony, and goodwill towards all. Keep your heart and mind open as you pursue your best version of self. Approach struggles from a standpoint of always willing to learn.

As we continuously work to align ourselves with God's Will while aspiring to live a life of Christian servitude, let us adopt the beliefs of becoming helpers and lifelong learners. Adopting these beliefs can create a better life for ourselves and others. Coexisting with others who think differently about life is an important life skill and part of being a Christian. Allow God to guide you to others whom you can connect with to help each other on your journey to accomplish your life purpose. Discern when to connect with others and when to let go with love. Take responsibility for yourself and your actions. You have control over one thing in this life—you. Focus on creating meaning and purpose through living a life of Christian servitude for God. Take control of yourself and be the best possible version of you, as you live a life of redefined intimacy

11

Peace, Love, and Goodwill

Where does your mind go when you have a quiet moment? What do you think about when you wake up in the morning? Our thoughts are connected, one leading to the other. If you begin a negative thought, your mind has a tendency to repeat that feeling with another negative thought. Before you know it, you are in a place where all of your thoughts are negative—a state of chaos. We need to become self-aware of our thoughts, and the reality of what we bring to conversation with others. Do you promote peace or chaos in your conversations?

As we mature from childhood into adulthood, we become more socially intelligent, and we tend to gravitate toward likeminded people. Any of us can find ourselves in a chaotic state at certain times in our lives. We take on new challenges as we attend school, meet new friends, As we transition from childhood to adulthood, we continue to explore the world beyond our childhood home. We may enter into a romantic relationship, start a career, raise children. Life events such as these can be great opportunities for personal growth and redefined intimacy in our life, but in the face of change, we can also experience a feeling of chaos. If you are overwhelmed with chaos in your life, please know that these things do not have to stay out of control. Many events that are prone to lend chaos are necessary milestones to feeling accomplished in life. These events are necessary to promote change and growth. Take a moment to ask God for help with any chaos you are experiencing.

As we grow older (read socially more mature), our lives start to slow down. It is as our schedules quiet down that our minds start to quiet down. In these quiet times, we have more opportunity for spiritual growth. Through discernment, we can learn how to draw conclusions from the challenges and events that occur in our lives. We think of new solutions, and make connections that we have previously been unaware. Furthermore, we can share these things with our family, friends, and co-workers. Sharing what we have learned allows people to discover our true beliefs. These beliefs define who we have become. As we share these beliefs with others in our intimate relationships, we also realize who we are. Do you know what your beliefs are—do you know who you are?

Coming to terms with who you are can also teach you who you are not. Now look at your intimate relationships. Are you able to be the best version of yourself and promote your best version to the others with whom you are intimate? Are your relationships helping you on your life journey to become more intimate with God, and more intimate with loved ones in your life?

You may be asking yourself, "So what types of relationships succeed the test of time?" The most successful relationships are those based in positive ideals. It is true that we can form bonds of love and trust through chaos and mutual hate, but as we discussed in chapters four and five, successful intimacy stems from love and trust. Love and trust are cultivated and grown over time through positivity. Chaos is experienced though busyness during life events that will not always exist. Bonding over mutual hate or dislike can also disappear, as people change. While it is true that God can take the chaotic events and turn them into opportunities to love, it is important to recognize what should be the basis for our healthy relationships. Peace, love, and goodwill are the basis for lasting and successful intimacies. These positive ideals can withstand the test of time.

As we mature, most of us realize that we want to avoid chaos. Antagonism has its place, and looking at life choices and struggles in terms of "the whole story" for the purpose of problem solving, brainstorming, and for cautionary measures can be important. Chaos and antagonism can be beneficial when offered with love for the purpose of personal growth, but so often they are rooted in fear and gossip. When focusing on building intimate relationships with other people, we want to build strong intimacy bonds based on trust and love, not antagonism and fear. Antagonism and fear are the opposite of constructive; they are deconstructive forces. We can stare the good, the bad, and the ugly in the face, but realize that most people will choose to gravitate toward the good. In order for relationships to last the test of time, they must be constructed of love and trust with a focus on creating peace, love, and goodwill.

How do we create these ideals of peace, love, and goodwill? By increasing our intimate relationship with God, we can hope to achieve these positive states of mind. As we share our worries and concerns with God and ask Jesus to carry them away, an amazing intimacy develops. God begins to heal our hearts. As our hearts heal, we learn the importance of becoming socially responsible, and promoting peace, love, and goodwill toward others.

Negative Nancy Family

Alita could not believe she was finally finished with her training program. She was so happy. She wanted to go out and mark the completion of this milestone with the ones she loved the most. After the ceremony, she took her family out to eat at her favorite restaurant. She began to get an ill-feeling in her stomach, as her family members were not offering support. Her younger sister joked that Alita would probably never get a job. When she cheerfully exclaimed that she had already received an offer and accepted it, her older sister told her that even though she had actually already received an offer, she probably was not going to make very much money. "Welcome to the real world, Sis!" Alita's aunt chimed in, suggesting, "You better go back to school now so you can make more money!" Alita stopped eating and stated, "I'm not hungry after all. Waiter, I'll take a to-go box and the check." Alita was looking forward to being alone. She loved her family, but she just didn't understand why they were never happy. She often felt like they drained the joy out of everything good, and that made it difficult for her to share her life with them. She silently wondered when she would feel like they were happy for her.

Have you ever been in a situation where you have felt like the moment did not live up to your expectations? In this story, Alita was taking her family out to say thank you, and to share in the celebration of completing a milestone in her life that was important to her on her life journey. While family and friends may have concerns about her wellbeing, it is always best to state concerns in a constructive way—with love. Perhaps stating your concerns at the celebration party is not the best time. Let's look at a different, more constructive way Alita's celebration party might occur:

Positive Pearl Family

Alita had just graduated from her training program after much hard work, and she really felt she had earned a well-deserved night out. She took her family to a nice restaurant to thank them for their support. Her sister asked her how she was going to look for jobs. "Are you looking at different data bases, or does your school help you look for jobs to start your career?" Alita happily exclaimed that she had already taken a job! After all, she felt that getting a job before she graduated was none too shabby of a feat, and she was brimming with joy about the prospect of starting her career. Her older sister said, "Congratulations, Sis! Let me know if I can offer you any advice about starting out; I have been through a first job before, and I am happy to help. But first, let's have a toast to your hard work and your well-deserved night out!"

"Know that we are always here for you if you need any help," said her quirky and favorite aunt. "You always have a home in our family. We are so proud of you for having the courage to accomplish this milestone on your life journey."

Which family dinner conversation would you rather be a part of? Both stories showed the family expressing concern for Alita, but they were markedly different. As she is just about to set off on her own, Alita's family is concerned that she will be financially secure and responsible. In the first story the family is creating chaos by stirring up fears. These are common fears that many of us have as we set off in a new phase in our lives. In the second story, the family is clearly radiating peace and love while exercising goodwill from their hearts, as they offer Alita help and support.

Life is not always as extreme as portrayed in these two stories of "Negative Nancy" and "Positive Pearl." These stories are only examples to illustrate a point. Which conversation would you rather be on the receiving end?

We are not always on our best behavior. Remember, we are not perfect. We are all sinners with fears, real life problems, and potential obstacles to our life satisfaction. Also, even though those in the first "Negative Nancy" story were dwelling on insecurity and life difficulties, it does not equal hating their sister. But it does lend itself to creating chaos and promoting a fear-centered mentality. Which of these statements is the most constructive way to support this intimate relationship in love and trust: "You better watch out," or "We are here for you."

As we go through our lives, we meet many "Negative Nancy's," "Positive Pearl's," and everyone in between. How often have you thought that your appetite has been soured because you had a conversation with someone in a bad mood? We have the power to spread chaos or peace, love or hate, and toxic thoughts or goodwill. We all have bad days, but what would you rather be responsible for promoting—love or hate?

Customer Service Nightmare

Dan was on the phone with customer service. He was really going to give them a piece of his mind! He was so upset that his refrigerator had stopped working in the first month!

"Good morning, this is Ronnie speaking. How can I direct your call this morning?"

Dan:

"Yeah, I am really disappointed. I bought a lemon of a refrigerator and I'm going to sue you."

Ronnie:

"Sir you sound upset. Can you tell me about your problem so I can direct you to a manager?"

Dan:

"Listen here! You are not hanging up on me. You are going to listen to what I have got to say because the customer is always right! When I say I bought a lemon, I mean it! You are not going to transfer me to someone else and put me on hold."

Ronnie:

"I understand you are upset sir. I want to make sure I get all the information so I can start your refund. Can you tell me the model number of the refrigerator you bought?"

Dan:

"I mean, come on, in this day and age, how does a new refrigerator even break? Don't they have machines making these things?"

Ronnie:

"Sir we don't make them here, we just sell them. Can you go ahead and give me the model number so I can get your claim started?"

Dan:

"You can look that up on your computer! I don't have to give you anything. I already gave you all the money for the refrigerator, and now you are going to give it back!"

Ronnie:

"I understand you are upset sir. I'll try to look it up by your name, but it will take longer that way. What is your last name?"

Dan:

"What do you mean it's going to take longer? I don't have all day!"

Ronnie:

"Would you like me to search by your name or the model number? The model number is located on a sticker on the inside of the refrigerator. I can help you find it if you tell me what kind of refrigerator you have. Or you can give me your last name, and I'll search all your transactions."

Dan:

"This is ridiculous! All of my food is defrosting and getting ruined! Are you going to reimburse me for my food that is in the refrigerator?"

Poor Ronnie. This is a painful conversation to hear, and even more so, it is painful to be on the receiving end of such a verbal assault and emotional unloading. In the story, Ronnie is doing a good job as a customer service representative. He is trying to maintain peace and calm in order to get his job done right, and more importantly get the customer what is needed. But Ronnie is met with opposition to get his job done. He is forced to listen to a rant from a dissatisfied customer who will not answer any of his questions. Even worse, Ronnie will be left with the footprint of chaos, hate, and hostility that he will need to overcome to get through the rest of his day. These are the types of moments that define us. When you experience negativity in the world, what do you tell yourself to get through these negative experiences?

What about Dan? Dan is really angry and his feelings are valid. He is probably also worried that the company is not going to return his money. It also appears that he may be embarrassed, because he secretly feels like he did a poor job of selecting the best and most reliable appliance. Dan is overwhelmed with emotions, and he is nervous about the outcome of receiving a refund. Everyone has the right to feel these ways, but no one has the right to take it out on an innocent person. Dan is exercising a fear tactic I like to call **grenading**.

A grenade is a handheld, explosive device that when triggered by the holder, can be thrown at a target and explode, throwing pieces of metal into the air at such a speed as to kill. If you think about Dan's verbal attack on Ronnie, you can hear the hateful words that Dan is shouting out of fear. Dan is causing hate rather than goodwill, and creating chaos rather than helping the situation come to a resolution. As a figure of speech, Dan is **grenading** Ronnie, throwing "verbal shrapnel" in an attempt to cause a distraction while Dan thinks of what to do and say next in his state of fear about losing his money. Ronnie is taking blow after blow, fighting through his emotional injury. Ronnie is trying to keep his positive ideals alive, or at the very least, he is trying to keep his job.

Think about a time in your life when you have been on the receiving end of a fear tactic like grenading. We have all experienced times in our lives when we have felt wronged, overwhelmed, and backed up into a corner. Now think about a time when you have been guilty of throwing out verbal shrapnel, grenading an innocent bystander when you are having a bad day, or are suffering from some other verbal, physical, or emotional abuse. Emotional violence is as real as physical violence. One violence can spill into another relationship creating a cycle of negativity.

Who has the power to change these vicious cycles of chaos, hate, and hostility? The answer is, you! In order to stop any cycle of negativity, you must first realize that you are playing a part. What type of footprint are you leaving behind on your journey to get to know God and others?

Let us work to promote a footprint of peace, love, and goodwill. As members of the community and social network, we all have a social responsibility to create peace rather than chaos, foster love as opposed to fear, and promote goodwill rather than hate. These are the ideals that allow intimate, meaningful relationships to flourish. Our desire for creating ideal relationships grows as our love for the Lord grows. I pray in this lifetime you achieve both an intimate relationship with God through Christ, as well as an intimate relationship with fellow sojourners along the way. If you desire more positivity in your intimate relationships, pray for God's guidance in bringing this into your reality.

Prayer for More Positivity

Dear God in the name of Jesus,

Please search me. I pray that you remove anything in my mind, body, and soul that is not serving you, Lord. Please remove any chaos, hate, and fear from my heart. I chose to allow you to heal me and fill my heart with the love of Jesus. Amen.

12

New Ground and Future Blessings

Intimacy (redefined) - the experience of God's love in your relationship with God and others in your life, whom God guides you to share His love; the fabric of a meaningful, happy, and satisfied life.

Throughout this book, we have been exploring what intimacy is, where to find it, and how to cultivate it. We have been slowly redefining what intimacy is in our relationships and what it can become. I hope that you have great hope and faith in the Lord that you can live your best reality possible. You are on your way to co-creating a reality full of meaning, purpose, and satisfaction, through redefined intimacy.

Discernment is an important and useful skill for attracting people interested in forming intimate relationships built on love and trust. Discernment is also a useful tactic for avoiding verbal shrapnel, or grenading. We can all have the ultimate goal of achieving and maintaining peace in our hearts, and yet be capable of speaking constructive criticism with love when we have disagreements and concerns. Discernment comes from God. Use discernment to help you create meaningful conversations and to increase the redefined intimacy in your life.

With whom should we attempt to establish intimacy? As we set out with the intention of living our life for God, people who God guides us to through Christian servitude are ideal candidates for intimate relationships. Ask God to guide you to people who will accept you for who you are now, as well as who you are becoming. Ask God to reform you in his image, making you a strong conduit for sending and receiving intimacy in meaningful relationships.

Which of your relationships are based on love, peace, and goodwill? It's possible that you have many relationships like this, or perhaps you want more relationships based on these things? Are there any relationships that can use some special attention? Ask God to help you discern which relationships need extra help, and perhaps which relationships you need to let go, with love in your heart, so both of you can continue to grow freely for God's plan.

What defense do we have against hate, fear, and chaos? Remember, we can only control ourselves; we cannot control other people or the spreading of hate, fear, and chaos by other people. The world can be filled with peace, love, and goodwill. We have a social responsibility to create and maintain these positive entities. Through our relationship with God, and getting to know him intimately, God can guide us on our life journey. He can help us live a life of Christian servitude that is full of intimacy, increasing meaningfulness, purpose, and satisfaction within all of our relationships.

You have the power to choose to live your best life now! You can live a fulfilling and meaningful life by creating a redefined intimacy with God and others. As we grow through life and experience different relationships, we learn that there is a natural hierarchy of relationships. Respecting the intimacy hierarchy ensures that we maintain healthy and positive connections to others in our lives throughout our lifetime. Sharing secret dreams and fears is reserved for the highest level of intimacy you can share with someone. However, this is the level of intimacy where satisfaction is reached in a relationship. This level of comfort and safety cannot be reached in just any relationship. You are blessed in your life when you reach this level of intimacy with someone else—whether it's a childhood friend you grew up with, a roommate you went through an important milestone or life event with, or a family member like a spouse, sibling or a parent. The ideal amount of intimacy we share with people is gauged by the desire that both people in the relationship have to be close, the time we have spent with them, the life events we have shared, and the trust that has been earned through these different situations.

Have you ever experienced a problem in your life that you felt you could not share with anyone? The embarrassment of a failure, the betrayal of a trusted love one, a crime of the world, or a crime of the heart? Feelings of fear and isolation deny us from true intimacy. The reality of life is that it may not feel right to share your problem with a loved one. Ask God, "Should I share this burden with my loved one?" By inviting God into the situation, we are opening our heart and allowing the Lord permission to guide us toward peace. Listen to the Lord's guidance. Another good way to determine if your burden is too much to share with someone else is if you try to share the problem or belief, and you witness your loved one shy away. These are the moments to recognize.

When life has gotten in the way of your peace, love, and goodwill, continue to ask for God's guidance. Help may best be achieved in these times of need by being outsourced to trusted professionals like counselors, ministers, and priests. These helping professionals can help you in your times of need as you invite God into your life situation.

In times of need, God wants us to know that we do not need to be alone. These are the times when the Lord wants us to take solace in Him, while asking for help in our world. Ask God, "Dear Lord, please send me someone in my time of need that I can confide in and trust to keep my secret while you heal me." You may be led to trained professionals, who are devoted to helping other people and working miracles that can help you in your time of need. God can work miracles in your life that you never thought possible. God can assist you in rebuilding intimate relationships with your loved ones; God can heal your heart to prepare you to be in a new, healthy, intimate relationship.

Feeling alone and isolated when you experience sadness, fear, anger, and pain is a strike from the Devil in a battle to steal our joy by dividing us from God and our other intimacies. When we feel these ways, this is an opportunity to go to God with the truth. Experience a redefined closeness with God as you share your truths and beliefs. Your intimacy will abundantly flourish as your desire to experience His unconditional love grows. We have explored many ways to experience God's Love as redefined intimacy. The following is a quick summary of how to invite God into your heart to experience redefined intimacy with God an others in your life.

God's Love as Redefined Intimacy

L—Lovingly invite God into your life problem and pain with the intention of sharing truths and fears with Him.

O—Open your heart to release to Him your anger, fears, sadness, and your pain as God fills the void that is left by these burdens.

V—Value the time you spend with the Lord and your relationship as you live a life of Christian servitude, expressing gratitude and glory to God for your blessings.

E—Experience the fruitful intimate relationships that develops from your intention to grow your relationship with God through faith, hope, and trust, and love.

Is your Volcano Heart overflowing with the desire to intimately know God? Do you desire to create a new reality, connecting you to others whom God guides you? I hope so. Envision your new reality of redefined intimacy in your life. Listening to Jesus in your Volcano Heart and enacting on the work that He guides you to perform will ensure God can create new ground for these meaningful relationships to grow. Here are some signs that you are ready to send and receive redefined intimacy in your life:

- You have a desire to be led into meaningful relationships with others. You focus on creating quality relationships, based on positivity and meaningful conversations.
- You respect other people's beliefs and differences, even when they are not your own.
- You uphold the freedom to hold different beliefs so everyone can learn and grow into the best version of self.
- You have an attitude of life-long learning rather than complacency with things you've already learned.

- You use discernment to decide when to engage in constructive criticisms or disagreements, and when to leave a situation or a relationship.
- You have decided to experience God's love, and now you have won a new ground for redefined intimacy in your life to grow and flourish.

For all of your future blessings, I pray that you win this new ground and redefined intimacy every day for the rest of your life. When you feel alone or isolated, look to Jesus within your heart. Allow God to heal you, so you can continue to experience meaningful relationships with intimacy, redefined.

Bibliography and Suggested Reading

Friend, G. *What's the Difference between Romance and Intimacy?* Internet source: drgaylefriend.com.

Goddard, D. (1996). *The Sacred Magic of the Angels.* Samuel Weiser, INC.

Keeney, B. (1987). *The Construction of Therapeutic Realities.* Psychotherapy. Volume 24/Fall 1987/Number 3S. Page 469-476.

Kendrick, A. (2015). *War Room.* Sony Pictures Releasing.

Kendrick, S. and Alex Kendrick. (2015). *The Battle Plan for Prayer: From Basic Training to Targeted Strategies.* B&H Publishing Group.

Kromberg, J. (2013). *The 5 Stages of Grieving the End of a Relationship*, psychologytoday.com.

McKean, E. (2005). *The New American Oxford Dictionary.* New York, N.Y.: Oxford University Press.

Marsh, S. *A Catholic Moment: Relief in our Servitude*, source-blog, aCatholic.org.

McLeod, S. (2009; 2015). *Freud and the Unconscious Mind.* simplypsychology.org

Moore, B. (2013). *Sacred Secrets: A Living Proof Live Experience.* Lifeway.

Schneider, K.A. (2014). *Do Not Be Afraid! How to Find Freedom from Fear.* Destiny Image. Publishers, Inc.

Schucman, Helen. (2007). *A Course In Miracles.* The Foundation for Inner Peace. 3rd Edition.

Truzy, T. (2019). *9 Bible Verses On Friendship,* holidappy.com, Dec 17, 2019.

Virtue, D. (1999). *Healing With the Angels: How the Angels Can Assist You in Every Area of Your Life.* New York, N.Y.: Hayhouse, Inc.

Wilson, B. (2020, March 9). *The Five Levels of Intimacy,* https://www.familylifecanada.com/blog/the-five-levels-of-intimacy/blog/.

Wicker, C. *Volcanos,* weatherwizkids.com.

Glossary

Active listening-listening with the intent of understanding.

Anchoring-pausing our journey to learn an important life lesson, or to allow for growth of ourselves or another person; a time for patience and reflection.

Christian servitude-devoting our purpose here on earth to serving God by following the ways and teachings of Jesus.

Commune-focus on God with great intensity; a sharing of heart and mind.

Discernment-spiritual guidance gained through intimacy with God and in the absence of judgment.

Gratitude-a state of thankfulness that comes from the heart; the highest experience of thankfulness.

Grenading-a fear tactic involving throwing verbal "shrapnel" in an attempt to cause a distraction in a state of feeling hurt or overwhelmed.

Intimacy (redefined)-the experience of God's love in your relationship with God and others in your life, whom God guides you to share His love.

Meaningful conversations-the threading of intimate bonds; open and accepting conversation with the purpose of gaining intimacy and catharsis through mutual understanding.

Politics-everything we do and say; activities.

Positivity-the practice or tendency of being positive.

Semantics-beliefs and the meaning we attribute to our beliefs.

Union-the choice to bring God with us on every step of our journey, even if we had left Him behind somewhere along the way; coming together with other people for the purpose of carrying out God's Will rather than your own free will.

www.ingramcontent.com/pod-product-compliance
Lightning Source LLC
Chambersburg PA
CBHW071455070526
44578CB00001B/343